11+ Verbal Reasoning

For the **CEM** test

This CGP book is brilliant for children aged 9-10 who are working towards the CEM 11+. It's set at a slightly easier level than the real test — perfect for building confidence.

The first few sections are packed with topic-based questions that'll help them get to grips with each crucial skill. Once they've mastered those, they can move on to the mixed-topic Assessment Tests for more realistic 11+ practice.

There are also detailed answers at the end to make marking as simple as possible!

How to access your free Online Edition

This book includes a free Online Edition to read on your PC, Mac or tablet. You'll just need to go to **cgpbooks.co.uk/extras** and enter this code:

0896 1680 2473 5865

By the way, this code only works for one person. If somebody else has used this book before you, they might have already claimed the Online Edition.

Practice Book – Ages 9-10
with Assessment Tests

How to use this Practice Book

This book is divided into two parts — themed question practice and assessment tests. There are answers with detailed explanations at the end of the book.

Themed question practice

- Each page has practice questions on a different theme. Use these pages to work out your child's strengths and the areas they find tricky. The questions get harder down each page.

- Your child can use the smiley face tick boxes to evaluate how confident they feel with each topic.

Assessment tests

- The second half of the book contains eight assessment tests, each with a mix of question types from the first half of the book.

- You can print multiple-choice answer sheets so your child can practise the tests as if they're sitting the real thing — visit cgpbooks.co.uk/11plus/answer-sheets or scan the QR code. →

- Use the printable answer sheets if you want your child to do each test more than once.

- If you want to give your child timed practice, give them a time limit of 25 minutes for each test, and ask them to work as quickly and carefully as they can.

- The tests get harder from 1-8, so don't be surprised if your child finds the later ones more tricky.

- Your child should aim for a mark of around 85% (48 questions correct) in each test. If they score less than this, use their results to work out the areas they need more practice on.

- If they haven't managed to finish the test in time, they need to work on increasing their speed, whereas if they have made a lot of mistakes, they need to work more carefully.

- Keep track of your child's scores using the progress chart on the inside back cover of the book.

- This book gives your child intensive practice of the Verbal Reasoning sections of the test. There will be other elements on the real 11+ test, such as Maths and Non-Verbal Reasoning.

- Although our question types are based on those set by CEM, we cannot guarantee that your child's actual 11+ exam will take the same format or contain the same question types as this book.

Published by CGP

Editors: Claire Boulter, Holly Poynton

Contributors: Jane Bayliss, Steve Martin, Lucy Towle

With thanks to Rebecca Tate and Luke von Kotze for the proofreading.

Please note that CGP is not associated with CEM in any way.
This book does not include any official questions and it is not endorsed by CEM.

ISBN: 978 1 78908 170 1

Printed by Elanders Ltd, Newcastle upon Tyne
Clipart from Corel®

Based on the classic CGP style created by Richard Parsons.

Contents

Tick off the check box for each topic as you go along.

Plurals

Plurals

Write the correct plural of the word in brackets.
Look at this example:

She loves riding __ponies__ (pony).

1. We had crunchy roast _____ (**potato**) with our Sunday lunch.

2. There were no _____ (**witness**) to the theft of the pocket watch.

3. The _____ (**leaf**) on the trees turn crimson and gold in autumn.

4. We saw the family of _____ (**fox**) who live at the bottom of our garden.

5. I've had three pet _____ (**canary**); the most recent one's called Boris.

6. Anouk is taking salmon _____ (**sandwich**) in her packed lunch.

7. My cousins consume six _____ (**loaf**) of bread every week.

8. They ordered twenty _____ (**pizza**) for the party.

/ 8

Plurals

Write the correct plural of the word in brackets.
Look at this example:

The theatre was crammed with noisy __children__ (**child**).

Hint: Say the plural word out loud to check that it sounds right.

9. The dentist declared that Susie's _____ (**tooth**) were healthy.

10. In Victorian times, only _____ (**man**) were allowed to vote.

11. We simply couldn't squeeze any more _____ (**person**) onto the train.

12. Sunesh was woken by the sound of three angry _____ (**goose**) honking in the yard.

13. Hygiene was so poor in the Middle Ages that many peasants had _____ (**louse**).

14. Marco's _____ (**foot**) were aching after the gruelling mountain walk.

15. I would like to purchase _____ (**this**) football boots.

16. We were chased by a flock of _____ (**sheep**) when we went for a picnic.

/ 8

Homophones

Homophones

Choose the correct homophone from the brackets.
Look at this example:

I have curly brown ___hair___ (**hare hair**).

1. We're having _____ (**our hour**) garage converted into a giant ball pool.

2. Her new bike had a _____ (**steal steel**) frame, so it was quite heavy.

3. Meredith had a new perfume which had an unusual _____ (**sent scent**).

4. I used too much _____ (**flour flower**), so my cake didn't rise.

5. These big cartons of milk are very hard to _____ (**poor pour**).

6. We sat on the dock and watched the boats _____ (**sail sale**) past.

7. When Keiko wore shorts, her _____ (**bear bare**) legs were bitten by mosquitoes.

8. Jon didn't have enough money for his bus _____ (**fair fare**).

9. We took the wrong _____ (**root route**) despite looking at the map.

10. The soles of my favourite trainers had _____ (**warn worn**) out.

/ 10

Homophones

Complete each sentence using **there**, **their** or **they're**.
Look at this example:

We're going to ___their___ house for Christmas.

11. Jakub is anxious about meeting my family, but _____ quite friendly really.

12. Chi was desperate to see _____ new ferret.

13. We play lacrosse on that pitch over _____.

14. When my dad was young, _____ was a huge reservoir here.

15. Polar bears clean _____ fur by rolling in the snow.

16. I don't know why _____ playing that terrible song.

/ 6

Section One — Spelling and Grammar

Prefixes and Suffixes

Prefixes

Add the prefix **in**, **im** or **il** to make each word negative.
Look at this example:

These maths questions are _im_ possible.

1. Katrin lost the debate because her argument was completely _____logical.

2. My little brother is really _____mature: he finds burping hilarious.

3. The con man was convicted of all sorts of _____legal activities.

4. The lead actor in the film was _____capable of stringing a sentence together.

5. Heidi knew her sketch was _____perfect, but she just couldn't get Dinah's nose right.

6. My sister spent an hour in the bathroom this morning; she's so _____considerate.

7. The giant rabbit enjoyed the novel even though the plot was totally _____plausible.

8. Kazuo would have got a better mark, but his writing is _____legible.

/ 8

Suffixes

Add the suffix **ment**, **ful** or **ness** to complete the word in brackets.
Look at this example:

The lake was always so __peaceful__ (**peace**) at dawn.

Hint: The spelling of the word may change when a suffix is added.

9. Cathy was planning to travel around the world during her _____ (**retire**).

10. Gulnar asked for Darren's _____ (**forgive**) when she broke his favourite mug.

11. The toolset was very _____ (**use**), but Kay wished they'd bought her a pony instead.

12. She received outstanding _____ (**treat**) during her illness.

13. Chandra gave up his chair for their guest out of _____ (**polite**).

14. The chefs reached an _____ (**agree**) about who was in charge of dessert.

15. We couldn't help but join in the _____ (**merry**).

16. Nina's _____ (**beauty**) new dress had glue all down the front.

/ 8

Section One — Spelling and Grammar

Awkward Spellings

Vowels

Add either **ie** or **ei** to form the words correctly.
Look at this example:

The path across the f_ie_ld was really muddy.

Hint: Remember the rule: 'i before e, except after c (but only when it rhymes with bee)'.

1. The jewel th_____f had stolen Lady Bunting's priceless diamond necklace.

2. The pr_____st came into school to talk to us about the harvest festival.

3. Kit asked for a rec_____pt in case his mum didn't like the tarantula he'd bought her.

4. Mrs Sharma's f_____rce dog barks at me every time I walk past her house.

5. Tiago asked for an extra large p_____ce of cake.

6. I don't like bubble baths and n_____ther does my cat.

7. The children were rel_____ved when they reached their destination.

8. I p_____rced the juice carton with the end of the straw.

/ 8

Consonants

Complete these words with the correct single or double consonant.
Look at this example:

The ra_bb_it scampered back to its burrow.

9. Art is brilliant, but my favourite lesson is hi_____tory.

10. Meera wasn't a_____owed sweets, except on special occasions.

11. When Paul gave Sara his a_____ress, he really hoped that she'd write to him.

12. We're jetting off on our holiday to Costa Rica to_____orrow!

13. Kell a_____epted Mo's apology for the mud-throwing incident.

14. The walrus wondered if it was really ne_____essary to wear the wetsuit Mum had bought him.

15. Stop what you're doing imme_____iately if the fire alarm goes off.

/ 8

16. Sophie finally su_____eeded in her quest to ban cabbage from school meals.

Section One — Spelling and Grammar

Mixed Spelling Questions

> Each sentence contains a spelling mistake. Underline the word with the error and write the correct spelling on the line.
> Look at this example:
>
> The chef grabbed his <u>knifes</u> and started chopping. ___knives___

Hint: If you can't spot the mistake straight away, look carefully at letter combinations that are often misspelt, such as double letters and plurals.

1. Hanna loved going to the field to feed the donkies.   _____

2. Mary made a meringue filled with cream and raspberrys.   _____

3. Miyako was startled by the sudden nock at the door.   _____

4. Sam wasn't sure which starecase led to the basement.   _____

5. Tiddles edged away from the empty fish tank, looking gilty.   _____

6. Parvani thought a ham and honey sanwich would be delicious.   _____   / 6

7. I thought the film was excellent; I'd definitely reccomend it.   _____

8. Marta's parents were very proud of there clever daughter.   _____

9. Remember to wiegh your ingredients when you're baking.   _____

10. The son was shining so we relaxed on the outdoor terrace.   _____

11. Our annual holiday in Cornwall was wonderfull.   _____

12. Paolo practised regularly ahead of the piano compitition.   _____   / 6

13. Vegetarians get protien from foods such as lentils and beans.   _____

14. Carl didn't actualy like jam tarts, but it seemed polite to eat one.   _____

15. Ian found that hopping was a very imefficient way to get around.   _____

16. Eric had a fine collection of novelty paper clips.   _____

17. The boys were bursting with excitment before they went skiing.   _____

18. The secratary was annoyed that she didn't have her own office.   _____   / 6

Section One — Spelling and Grammar

Mixed Spelling Questions

Underline the correct word to complete each sentence.
Look at this example:

I went to the shop to **(<u>buy</u> by)** some milk.

1. **(To Too)** many people, Kate was an excellent role model.

2. The puppy got **(to too)** excited and knocked over the precious statue.

3. I don't know **(whether weather)** to go for a bike ride today.

4. The zombie wanted to go hiking, but the **(whether weather)** forecast wasn't very good.

5. "Please may I **(lend borrow)** your protractor?" asked Hamsa.

6. "Only if you **(lend borrow)** me your green pen," answered Rhiannon.

/ 6

7. I couldn't **(where wear)** my football shirt because it was covered in mud.

8. Jamelia suddenly remembered **(where wear)** she had left her keys.

9. There's nothing **(worse worst)** than sandy food at the beach.

10. I am the **(worse worst)** snooker player in the entire family.

11. Max thought he had done **(well good)** in his saxophone exam.

12. Chunni was **(well good)** at making new friends, so she had a busy social life.

/ 6

13. I was devastated to **(loose lose)** the cross-country race.

14. I forgot to wear socks, so my shoes were very **(loose lose)**.

15. I'm extremely full but I've got a craving for the lemon **(desert dessert)**.

16. He had wandered for days through the barren **(desert dessert)** with no water.

17. That's the man **(which who)** tried to sell me a luminous inflatable pinboard.

18. I bought two polka-dot shirts, **(which who)** used up all my pocket money.

/ 6

Section One — Spelling and Grammar

Verbs

Verbs

Underline the correct verb from the brackets to complete each sentence. Look at this example:

Andy **(i<u>s</u> were be)** going to the park today.

1. Cerys **(went goes gone)** to the doctor's last night.

2. Blacksmiths have **(making make made)** horseshoes for centuries.

3. Divyesh is **(have going having)** a bouncy-castle party on Sunday afternoon.

4. I **(was is had)** just finishing my homework when the doorbell rang.

5. "It has **(broken broke break)**!" cried Mahmud mournfully.

6. The sailor **(talk talked talks)** until the sun rose about his time at sea.

/ 6

7. Grace had **(fell fall fallen)** over and landed in the mud.

8. Corned beef makes me **(feel feeling felt)** ill.

9. He **(drives driven drove)** to school in a go-kart yesterday.

10. My nephew always **(laughs laughed laugh)** when I tickle him.

11. I **(sees saw seen)** where the group of runners went.

12. It **(is were was)** forbidden to enter the courtyard when the gate was shut.

/ 6

13. He **(hears hear heard)** the steam train before he could see it.

14. Salami **(is are were)** a type of cured meat eaten with bread.

15. Lottie watched the spider **(spin spun spins)** its web.

16. The choir had **(sang sings sung)** the piece many times before.

17. Once Ben **(begins begun began)** writing the story, he couldn't stop.

18. I **(bought brought buys)** these apples at the market.

 / 6

Section One — Spelling and Grammar

Verbs and Conjunctions

Verbs

Change the verb in bold so that it is in the correct tense.
Look at this example:

Kim **gone** to karate class last Sunday.   _went_

1. Matt still gets annoyed when people **didn't** tidy up.   _____

2. Beth felt quite travel sick when she **flies** to Australia.   _____

3. I **go** to the theme park with my cousins yesterday.   _____

4. He was annoyed when the dog **knocks** over his drink.   _____

5. My dad can **spoke** six languages, including Mandarin.   _____

6. My goldfish was delighted when she **passes** her driving test.   _____

7. I **leave** my P.E. kit in the changing rooms last week.   _____

8. "Take that back!" **say** Amara as she slammed the door.   _____

/ 8

Conjunctions

Underline the most appropriate conjunction from the brackets to complete each sentence.
Look at this example:

I like your tortoise **(if <u>but</u> unless)** I prefer my hamster.

9. I don't want to come to the park, **(because so or)** it is snowing.

10. Hand me the hammer **(if so though)** I can hang this picture.

11. Over the weekend, I went swimming **(but and since)** I went ice skating.

12. Put your coat on **(yet since before)** you leave the house.

13. We can have our pudding now **(or but when)** we can wait until later.

14. Don't open your present **(until when while)** your mum arrives.

15. Maisie went to school **(whereas nor or)** her brother stayed at home.

16. You can't come in **(or unless whereas)** you've brought cake.

/ 8

Section One — Spelling and Grammar

Mixed Grammar Questions

Each sentence has one grammatical error. Underline the word which is wrong and write the correct word on the line.
Look at this example:

Rachel rushed over to <u>helps</u>.   _help_

1. Aisha enjoyed cycling quick around the duck pond.   _____

2. We decided to ate our picnic under the large beech tree.   _____

3. I saw the ginger kitten when he were prowling in the garden.   _____

4. Us travelled to Hawaii with our pet mouse.   _____

5. Are you going to swam across the English Channel?   _____

6. I don't want no chips with my burger.   _____

7. When I were five, I fell out of a bedroom window.   _____

8. Melinda (the woman with blonde hair) is mine sister-in-law.   _____   / 8

Write down whether the word in bold is a noun, verb, conjunction, adjective or adverb. Look at this example:

He **works** at the weekends.   _verb_

9. The caring **nurse** tended to her infirm patient.   _____

10. Last night, I **danced** the tango and the rumba with Alejandro.   _____

11. **Listen** carefully to all the instructions before you begin.   _____

12. He is an **impressive** chess player, but he won't beat Peter.   _____

13. **Suddenly** the boat capsized and we were thrown into the water.   _____

14. I don't know the answer — can I have a **clue**?   _____

15. You stand guard **while** I get the chocolates.   _____

16. He pulled the rope **quickly** to tighten the tarpaulin over the car.   _____   / 8

Multiple Meanings

Choose the word that has a similar meaning to the words in both sets of brackets. Underline your answer.

Look at this example:

(serious solemn) (burial tomb)   coffin gloomy <u>grave</u>

Hint: The answer might be pronounced differently for the two different meanings.

1. (sugary syrupy)   (lovely kind)   candy nice sweet

2. (drama show)   (romp frolic)   play musical actor

3. (snug cramped)   (mean stingy)   unfair tight poor

4. (summit peak)   (lid cap)   mountain hat top

5. (overturn spill)   (bother worry)   roll upset ask

6. (chilly icy)   (unfriendly aloof) cold mean freezing

/ 6

7. (plain natural)   (easy clear)   straight simple hard

8. (now current)   (gift offering)   ask present past

9. (class set)   (application questionnaire) type school form

10. (nice tender)   (type sort)   group keep kind

11. (game contest)   (pairing partnership) match sport union

12. (autograph initial) (poster notice)   banner write sign

/ 6

13. (instant moment) (runner-up next)   day race second

14. (important major) (guide code)   key idea primary

15. (group orchestra) (ring circle)   band music join

16. (rubbish garbage) (deny decline)   trash refuse bin

17. (argue fight)   (paddle sail)   row swim bicker

18. (pig boar)   (seed plant)   piglet grow sow

/ 6

Closest Meaning

Find the word that means the same, or nearly the same, as the word on the left. Underline your answer.

Look at this example:

talk   joke hum <u>chat</u> listen

1. **angry**   cross excited scared glare

2. **kind**   smile laugh nice quiet

3. **buy**   sell aim lend purchase

4. **ugly**   hideous sour surly scary

5. **allow**   refuse permit tidy given

6. **whisper**   talk laugh murmur silence

/ 6

7. **funny**   laugh annoying amusing sweet

8. **litter**   clean garbage dust bin

9. **precious**   valuable poor worthy lovely

10. **honest**   forgetful sorry truthful real

11. **rain**   snow storm downpour tornado

12. **same**   different identical related even

/ 6

13. **wish**   hope fear imagine like

14. **graph**   draw shape chart numbers

15. **cunning**   nasty vicious irritable sly

16. **friendly**   amiable dream wishful dour

17. **tidy**   clean cluttered neat slovenly

18. **forgive**   release pardon censure apologise

Hint: The word you choose doesn't have to mean exactly the same as the word on the left — it just has to be the most similar of all the options.

/ 6

Section Two — Word Meanings

Closest Meaning

Complete the word on the right so that it means the same, or nearly the same, as the word on the left.

Look at this example:

glad ⬚ h a p p y

1. **large**   v ⬚ ⬚ t
2. **hot**   ⬚ o ⬚ ⬚ i n g
3. **cry**   w e ⬚ ⬚
4. **stop**   f i ⬚ ⬚ s ⬚
5. **fall**   p ⬚ u ⬚ g ⬚
6. **fake**   f ⬚ ⬚ s e

Hint: Some words can mean more than one thing — e.g. 'close' means 'shut' and 'nearby'. If you're stuck, think about other meanings of the word.

/ 6

7. **cold**   c ⬚ i ⬚ ⬚ y
8. **plump**   c ⬚ u ⬚ b y
9. **good**   s ⬚ p ⬚ ⬚ b
10. **love**   ⬚ d o r ⬚
11. **tell**   i ⬚ ⬚ ⬚ r m
12. **weird**   s ⬚ ⬚ a ⬚ ⬚ e

/ 6

13. **question**   q ⬚ ⬚ ⬚ y
14. **bad**   d ⬚ ⬚ ⬚ d ⬚ ⬚ l
15. **rough**   c ⬚ a ⬚ s ⬚
16. **angry**   ⬚ u r i ⬚ ⬚ ⬚
17. **short**   b ⬚ ⬚ ⬚ f
18. **brave**   d ⬚ ⬚ i ⬚ ⬚

/ 6

Section Two — Word Meanings

14

Opposite Meaning

Find the word that means the opposite, or nearly the opposite, of the word on the left. Underline your answer.

Look at this example:

dark   night   <u>light</u>   cold   dusk

1. **upstairs**   cellar   downstairs   hall   landing

2. **clean**   neat   chaotic   filthy   trim

3. **young**   crooked   mean   modern   old

4. **beautiful**   boring   repulsive   harsh   enticing

5. **full**   bloated   slim   large   empty

6. **wide**   narrow   high   tapering   broad

Hint: If you're not sure what a word means, look it up in the dictionary.

/ 6

7. **love**   ignore   sad   loathe   lonely

8. **deep**   buried   shallow   stream   beneath

9. **shiny**   dull   old   soft   glazed

10. **stretch**   chop   slice   roll   squash

11. **poor**   famous   lonely   wealthy   greedy

12. **sell**   borrow   deal   pay   buy

/ 6

13. **minor**   much   major   large   part

14. **cheap**   costly   rich   bargain   excessive

15. **enemy**   guest   foe   friend   mentor

16. **busy**   silent   quiet   peace   crowded

17. **taut**   undone   snug   free   slack

18. **bumpy**   flat   rugged   stretched   regular

/ 6

Section Two — Word Meanings

Opposite Meaning

Complete the word on the right so that it means the opposite, or nearly the opposite, of the word on the left.

Look at this example:

right   [w][r][o][n][g]

1. **whole**   [p][a][ ][ ][a][l]
2. **alive**   [d][e][ ][ ][s][e][d]
3. **slow**   [ ][ ][i][ ][k]
4. **shout**   [w][ ][i][ ][ ][e][r]
5. **shy**   [b][o][ ][ ]
6. **take**   [d][ ][ ][ ][t][e]

> **Hint:** If you can't spot the word straight away, look for common letter patterns like 'qu' at the start of a word or 'ck' at the end.

/ 6

7. **quiet**   [ ][o][ ][ ][y]
8. **problem**   [s][ ][ ][u][ ][o][n]
9. **different**   [ ][t][a][n][ ][ ][ ][d]
10. **rare**   [c][ ][ ][ ][o][n]
11. **question**   [r][ ][ ][p][o][ ][d]
12. **past**   [f][ ][ ][u][ ][ ]

/ 6

13. **clear**   [c][ ][ ][ ][d][y]
14. **rude**   [p][ ][ ][i][ ][e]
15. **shorten**   [e][ ][t][ ][ ][d]
16. **close**   [d][ ][ ][ ][a][n][t]
17. **straight**   [ ][ ][r][v][ ][d]
18. **destroy**   [c][ ][e][ ][t][ ]

/ 6

Section Two — Word Meanings

Odd One Out

Three of the words in each list are linked. Underline the word that is not related to these three.

Look at this example:

<u>Tom</u>   Kate   Jenny   Lucy

1. numbers   five   eleven   seven

2. freezing   warm   chilly   cold

3. like   hate   love   admire

4. shout   mutter   yell   scream

5. house   bungalow   office   flat

6. woodland   glacier   rainforest   orchard

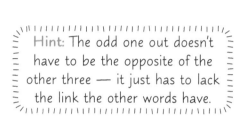

Hint: The odd one out doesn't have to be the opposite of the other three — it just has to lack the link the other words have.

 / 6

7. rose   daffodil   lily   oak

8. cooker   oven   fridge   microwave

9. football   slide   cricket   rugby

10. violin   harp   recorder   guitar

11. scarf   shorts   coat   mittens

12. happy   glad   pleased   chuckle

/ 6

13. shoes   socks   gloves   slippers

14. roast   diced   boiled   baked

15. sketch   portrait   song   drawing

16. wool   leather   cotton   plastic

17. sing   rehearsal   recite   dance

18. exit   leave   come   go

/ 6

Reorder Words to Make a Sentence

Rearrange the words so that each sentence makes sense.
Underline the word which doesn't fit into the sentence.

Look at this example:

enjoy tennis I playing <u>net</u> Tom with

The remaining words can be arranged into the sentence:
I enjoy playing tennis with Tom.

1. is season my favourite snow winter

2. school stables donkey rode to I on a

3. this read homework for book pages your

4. look ways cross traffic when both you road the

5. Maths study subjects are Science and my favourite

6. the darted table wooden run cat under the

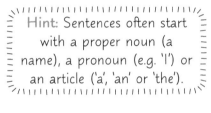

Hint: Sentences often start with a proper noun (a name), a pronoun (e.g. 'I') or an article ('a', 'an' or 'the').

/ 6

7. last we France in camping went tent summer

8. laces on socks your shoes put before your

9. learn I to foreign Italian want speak to

10. apple ogre red crunch on a the munched

11. circus watch the opens night tomorrow

12. whistle his blew referee at the the end pitch

/ 6

13. we time there will not it station make on

14. Eric we have mongoose a has pet called

15. the sailed ran gracefully barge canal the down

16. go Gemma early up got to wrestling morning

17. journey bus I am the taking school to tomorrow

18. postman office carried of letters the bag his

/ 6

Section Two — Word Meanings

Using Rules of English

> Underline the most appropriate word from the brackets to complete each sentence. Look at this example:
>
> Brian went out **(<u>because</u> despite to during)** it had stopped raining.

1. I am going to watch TV **(during so yet until)** Nassrin arrives.

2. When I forgot my pen, Zane said I could **(borrowed borrow borrows lend)** one of his.

3. He **(slowly fast quick slower)** raised his hand to answer the question.

4. Luke used to **(love loved loves enjoyed)** eating pancakes for breakfast.

5. I was grateful for his **(thought thoughtful thinking thoughts)** present.

6. I always wondered **(that what which when)** lay beyond the mansion's gates.

/ 6

7. I **(finding found find finds)** the day at the museum interesting.

8. When we made paper lanterns, the glue **(sticks sticky stuck sticked)** to my fingers.

9. We had to pass **(through around into on)** a security scanner to reach the departure lounge.

10. Of all my friends, I know you the **(well best good better)**.

11. Tamara won the medal; it was **(their hers her its)** third victory this year.

12. I cracked the egg **(into through around to)** the cake batter.

/ 6

13. My teacher looked **(seriously serious angrily seriousness)** when he told me to stop talking.

14. When my family go on holiday, we take **(our their are ours)** own towels.

15. **(During Although Despite However)** I had a fever, I came first in the egg-and-spoon race.

16. Marc threw the ball, and then the whistle blew; the trophy was **(their theirs they're these)**.

17. Manjit **(bought brought bring buys)** crisps and sandwiches to the garden party.

18. This week's play was **(longer lengthy longest long)** than last week's.

/ 6

Choose a Word

Choose the correct words to complete each passage below.

Marco waited
1. ☐ nervously
☐ hurriedly   at the side of the pool. Five other swimmers were
☐ victoriously

2. ☐ lines
☐ line   up next to him. He snapped his goggles on and
☐ lining

3. ☐ spent
☐ took   a deep breath.
☐ gasped

He had to win this race
4. ☐ if
☐ but   his school was to stay in the competition.
☐ since

/ 4

The tallest building in the world is
5. ☐ usually
☐ completely the Burj Khalifa in Dubai.
☐ currently

6. ☐ Complete
☐ Completes in 2009, it
☐ Completed

7. ☐ measures
☐ ranges   over 828 m — almost twice the
☐ scales

8. ☐ price
☐ big   of the Empire State Building.
☐ height

/ 4

Martial arts were
9. ☐ never
☐ first   practised over 4,000 years ago in ancient China. Today, there
☐ always

are many
10. ☐ reasons
☐ patterns   why martial arts are popular. Some people practise martial arts to
☐ suggestions

stay
11. ☐ brave
☐ happy , while others find that it helps their coordination and
☐ fit

12. ☐ knowledge
☐ skills   .
☐ balance

/ 4

20

Choose a Word

Choose the correct words to complete each passage below.

Ancient Romans took their food very

1.
☐ patiently
☐ suspiciously
☐ playfully
☐ seriously

, and wealthy citizens would hold

2.
☐ tasteless
☐ lavish
☐ paltry
☐ extreme

feasts for their guests.

3.
☐ Until
☐ If
☐ Although
☐ Yet

you were a guest at a Roman feast,

you might have been

4.
☐ poured
☐ shown
☐ presented
☐ served

dormouse, peacock or even a pig's ear. Despite these

unusual dishes, many ingredients used in Roman cooking are still

5.
☐ delicious
☐ edible
☐ popular
☐ tasted

today.

/ 5

Jennifer opened her curtains and gazed

6.
☐ to
☐ in
☐ at
☐ through

the glistening white carpet that

covered the ground below her

7.
☐ door
☐ wall
☐ roof
☐ window

. The garden path was

8.
☐ hidden
☐ hide
☐ hides
☐ hid

under

a frosty blanket of snow, and sparkling icicles

9.
☐ swung
☐ slid
☐ dangled
☐ broke

from the shed roof. Her heart

leapt with

10.
☐ dismay
☐ confusion
☐ glee
☐ sadness

. This could only mean one thing: no school today!

/ 5

Section Three — Completing Passages

 ✓ ✓ ✓

Fill in Missing Letters

Fill in the missing letters to complete the words in the following passages.

1. Pupils and teachers at Mossbridge School have ra◯◯◯d over £500 for their

2. local hospital after a s◯cces◯◯ul summer fair. The fair was held on the

3. school playing f◯◯ld last Saturday. It was the busiest event the school has ever

4. seen, attracting over 200 v◯s◯t◯rs . There was a wide range of attractions,
    including a cake stall selling cupcakes, a welly-tossing game and a raffle with a

5. variety of great pr◯z◯s . Headteacher Miss Martin said, "It was a

6. bri◯◯◯ant day and we've raised lots of money for a worthy cause."

/ 6

7. In this c◯◯◯try , four-leaved clovers and horseshoes are traditionally meant

8. to bring good luck. ◯th◯r countries and cultures have their own lucky

9. symbols. In China, the number 8 is meant to bring good fo◯◯◯ne —

10. that's why the 2008 Olympic Games, held in China's c◯pi◯◯l city, Beijing,
    started at 8 minutes past 8 o'clock on the 8th of August 2008. The Vikings

11. thought that acorns were lucky, and that they would p◯◯vent a

12. home from being st◯◯◯k by lightning.

/ 6

13. The c◯◯◯k struck six and, having swept up the hearth, Beth put a pair of

14. s◯ip◯◯rs down to warm. Somehow the sight of the old shoes had a good

15. effect upon the girls, for Mother was coming, and ever◯◯◯e brightened

16. to welcome her. Meg st◯◯pe◯ lecturing, and lighted the lamp, Amy got

17. out of the easy chair without being asked, and Jo fo◯◯◯t how tired

18. she was as she sat up to hold the slippers n◯◯rer to the blaze.

/ 6

From 'Little Women' by Louisa May Alcott

Section Three — Completing Passages

22

Fill in Missing Letters

Fill in the missing letters to complete the words in the following passages.

On Sunday 2nd September 1666, a fire broke out in a bakery on Pudding Lane.

1. Like most of the b☐☐ld☐ngs in London at the time, the bakery was made from
2. ti☐☐☐r and thatch, and the fire quickly spread through the bakery and the
3. ne☐☐☐bouring structures. Soon the whole of Pudding Lane was alight, and
4. the fire became unc☐☐trol☐able . Fanned by strong winds, the fire raged
5. thr☐☐g☐ the city for nearly five days, burning almost everything in
6. its path. This tra☐☐☐y became known as the Great Fire of London.

/ 6

In 1924, a professor at a university in Tokyo, Japan, owned a dog called Hachiko.

7. Every day for over a year, the professor would ☐a☐ch a train to work in the
8. morning, and in the ev☐☐in☐ Hachiko would go to the station and wait for his
9. ☐☐☐ter to return. In 1925, the professor died while he was at work; he never
10. made the return ☐ou☐ne☐ to the station. Every day for almost 10 years,
11. Hachiko ☐ait☐☐ at the station for the professor. Almost 90 years
12. later, Hachiko is still remembered in Japan for his lo☐☐☐☐y .

/ 6

13. Alice opened the door and fo☐☐d that it led into a small passage, not much
14. larger than a rat-hole: she ☐☐elt down and looked along the passage into the
15. loveliest garden you ever saw. How she lo☐☐☐d to get out of that dark hall,
16. and w☐nde☐ about among those beds of bright flowers and those cool
17. fountains, but she could not even get her head through the d☐☐☐☐ay ; 'and

even if my head would go through,' thought poor Alice, 'it would be of very little

18. use without my sh☐☐l☐ers . Oh, how I wish I could shut up like

a telescope!'

From 'Alice's Adventures in Wonderland' by Lewis Carroll

/ 6

Finding Hidden Facts

> Read the information carefully, and then use it to answer the question that follows. Write your answer on the line.

Hint: Some questions contain lots of information — write it in a grid to help you answer the question.

1. Jane, Debbie, Victoria, Lisa and Pierre all enjoy horse riding.

   Everyone except Victoria rides on Saturday. Pierre rides after school on Monday.
   Only Lisa and Victoria ride on Sunday morning. Lisa also rides on Wednesday.

   Who goes riding **most** often?   _____

2. Alice, Grace, Rana, Mark and William are all going on holiday this year.

   Grace and Rana are going on an activity holiday. Mark is going to Ireland.
   Alice is going to a hotel in France. Rana, Grace and Alice are going camping.
   William is going on a cycling holiday in Devon with Mark.

   Who is going on the **fewest** holidays?   _____

3. Haj, Jason, Georgia, Rosie and Lucy all like pizza, especially with unusual toppings.

   Everyone likes raisins, except Jason and Lucy. Jason's favourite topping is baked beans.
   Georgia and Haj eat lemon curd on their pizza. Lucy and Haj both like sausages.

   Who likes the **most** toppings on their pizza?   _____

4. James, Edward, Ellie, Shreena and Alec are talking about their plans for the weekend.

   Ellie, Edward and James are all going swimming. Alec and Shreena are visiting family.
   Ellie and Shreena plan to go to the cinema. The boys are going shopping.
   Everyone except Edward plans to go to the park.

   Who has the **fewest** plans for the weekend?   _____

   / 4

Multiple-Statement Questions — Logic

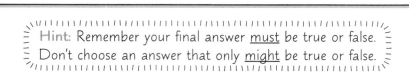

Read the information carefully, and then use it to answer the question that follows. Underline the correct answer.

Hint: Remember your final answer <u>must</u> be true or false. Don't choose an answer that only <u>might</u> be true or false.

1. Max, Charlotte, Ahmed and Victoria all attend a running club. Max runs faster than Charlotte. Victoria runs faster than Max. Ahmed is slower than Charlotte.

   If these statements are true, only one of the sentences below **must** be true. Which one?

   A Charlotte runs faster than Victoria.

   B Ahmed is quicker than Victoria.

   C Max is the fastest runner.

   D Max runs faster than Ahmed.

2. Sophie, Karl, Daisy, Josh and Abbie are talking about their houses. Sophie lives in a house with three bedrooms. Karl and Daisy both live in houses with more bedrooms than Sophie's. Abbie's house doesn't have a garden. Josh's house has half as many bedrooms as Karl's.

   If these statements are true, only one of the sentences below **cannot** be true. Which one?

   A Daisy lives in a house with four bedrooms.

   B Karl's house has five bedrooms.

   C Daisy's house is bigger than Abbie's.

   D Josh has his own bedroom.

3. Laura, Georgia, Rohan and Jamie were all born in August. Georgia was born before Laura, but after Jamie. Rohan was born after Jamie.

   If these statements are true, only one of the sentences below **must** be true. Which one?

   A Laura is older than Georgia.

   B Georgia was born on the same day as Rohan.

   C Laura is older than Rohan.

   D Jamie is the oldest.

/ 3

Multiple-Statement Questions — Logic

> Read the information carefully, and then use it to answer the
> question that follows. Underline the correct answer.

4. Last year, the average temperature in August was 2 degrees hotter than in June. The average
temperature in June was 15 degrees Celsius — that was 7 degrees less than July's average.
The coldest day in September was 8 degrees cooler than August's average.

   If these statements are true, only one of the sentences below **cannot** be true. Which one?

   A The average temperature in July was 22 degrees Celsius.

   B The coldest day in September was 9 degrees.

   C July was hotter than June.

   D July was cooler than August.

5. Patrick, Angharad, Hannah, Jacob and Sushmita all need to catch buses to meet in town.
Jacob's bus arrives 15 minutes after Hannah's bus. Sushmita's bus arrives 20 minutes before
Angharad's. Patrick's bus arrives at 7.15pm. Hannah's bus arrives 10 minutes after Patrick's.

   If these statements are true, only one of the sentences below **must** be true. Which one?

   A Hannah's bus arrives at 7.30pm.

   B Jacob's bus arrives at 7.40pm.

   C Patrick and Sushmita arrive at the same time.

   D Sushmita arrives at 7.50pm.

6. Lily, Charlie, Grace, Lucy and Dan are given money to spend on attracting visitors to their school
fair. Charlie spends more than £10. Together, Grace and Dan spend £20 on paint. Lucy buys
four banners for £3 each. Dan's paint costs £6.50. Lily spends half as much as Lucy.

   If these statements are true, only one of the sentences below **must** be true. Which one?

   A Charlie spends more than Grace.

   B Dan spends the same amount as Grace.

   C Grace spends more than Lily.

   D Lucy spends the most money.

/ 3

26

Understanding the Language in the Text

> Read the passage below, and then answer the questions that follow.
> Underline the correct option for each question.

1   Haji woke with a start. The curtains whispered in the breeze and, when he peered out
from under the dark cave of his duvet, he could see two dimly glowing lights hovering
beneath his desk.

"Khalid," he hissed, "are you awake?"

5   There was a groan from the other side of the room as his twin brother stirred. "Go back
to sleep, Haji," he mumbled groggily. "It's just a nightmare." Within seconds he was quietly
snoring again.

Haji, however, couldn't fall asleep so easily. The pair of lights seemed to be getting closer
and he could make out a low rumble, like the growl of a strange animal. He suddenly felt very

10 scared; his heartbeat was a drum thumping inside his chest.

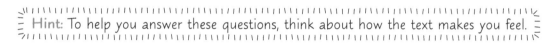
Hint: To help you answer these questions, think about how the text makes you feel.

1.   The author says that Haji's duvet is a "cave" (line 2). This shows that his duvet is:
     A very cold and dark.   **B** made of rock.   **C** shaped like a cave.

2.   The author says that Haji "hissed" (line 4). Why do you think Haji does this?
     A He's angry.   **B** He's in pain.   **C** He doesn't want to make much noise.

3.   The author says that Haji's heartbeat was a "drum thumping inside his chest" (line 10).
     This shows that:
     A his heartbeat was loud.   **B** he was playing the drums.   **C** his heartbeat was quiet.

4.   "The curtains whispered in the breeze" (line 1).
     What does this tell you about how the curtains moved?
     A They moved softly.   **B** They moved quickly.   **C** They moved constantly.

5.   The author compares the noise Haji hears to the "growl of a strange animal" (line 9).
     What does this suggest about whatever is making the noise?
     A It's friendly.   **B** It's dangerous.   **C** It's sleeping.

    / 5

Section Four — Comprehension

    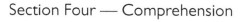

Mixed Comprehension Questions

Read the passage below, and then answer the questions that follow.

1   Today, Rome is the capital city of Italy, but 2,000 years ago it was the centre of the
Roman Empire. The Roman Empire was the name given to the lands ruled by the Emperor; at
its peak, it stretched from England to Egypt. One such Emperor was Hadrian, the man who
was responsible for building Hadrian's Wall. Hadrian's Wall was built near England's border
5   with Scotland, marking the northernmost boundary of the Roman Empire. Construction
started about 1900 years ago and took about six years. Made from limestone, earth and clay,
the wall was 3-6 metres high. At around 117 kilometres long, it's still the longest wall in
Europe, although many parts have fallen into disrepair.

The reasons for building Hadrian's Wall are unclear. Some historians believe it was
10   built to stop invaders from North Britannia (Scotland), but others think it was used to control
immigration and smuggling and to tax goods. Another theory is that it was built to show off
Rome's might, as it could be seen for miles around.

Around 9,000 soldiers were needed to man the wall. These soldiers lived in large forts
which had temples, granaries, bath houses and even hospitals. Apart from occasional attacks
15   from the north, life on the wall was mostly peaceful.

After Hadrian's death, Emperor Antoninus Pius abandoned Hadrian's Wall and built
the Antonine Wall, 160 kilometres further north. Antoninus believed that it would help
the Romans conquer Scotland, but his efforts were fruitless, and when he died the soldiers
retreated to Hadrian's Wall. The Romans left Britain around 1600 years ago, and by 1200
20   years ago people had already started to reuse the stones from the wall in roads and other
buildings, such as the monastery at Jarrow.

Turn over for the questions

Mixed Comprehension Questions

> Answer these questions about the text on page 27.
> Circle the letter of the correct option for each question.

1. Which of the following best describes how the wall looks today?
   A Fully intact
   B Buried
   C Demolished
   D Partially broken down

2. What did Hadrian's Wall mark?
   A The English border
   B The Scottish border
   C The northern border of the Roman Empire
   D Hadrian's kingdom

3. The Roman forts near the wall had many facilities, but which of the following are not mentioned in the text?
   A Places of worship
   B Tax offices
   C Storage for grain
   D Washing facilities

4. During the Roman period, Hadrian's Wall was:
   A attacked by the English.
   B often fought over.
   C sometimes attacked.
   D never attacked.

5. Why was the Antonine Wall constructed?
   A To re-use stones from Hadrian's Wall
   B To replace Hadrian's Wall
   C To protect the Roman Empire from invaders from the north
   D To extend the Roman Empire to the north

/ 5

Mixed Comprehension Questions

> Answer these questions about the text on page 27.
> Circle the letter of the correct option for each question.

6. Which one of the following is not suggested as a
    reason why Hadrian's Wall was built?
    A To tax produce
    B To demonstrate how powerful Rome was
    C To stop attackers
    D To increase immigration

7. Which of these statements about Hadrian's Wall is not mentioned in the passage?
    A It's the longest wall in the world.
    B It took less than 10 years to build.
    C It took around 9,000 soldiers to occupy the wall.
    D You can still see parts of the wall today.

8. In the context of the passage, what does the word "might" (line 12) mean?
    A Maybe
    B Ability
    C Power
    D Command

9. What does the word "retreated" (line 19) mean?
    A Withdrew
    B Abandoned
    C Escaped
    D Defended

10. What is the meaning of the phrase "his efforts were fruitless" (line 18)?
    A He made a lot of mistakes.
    B He didn't get the credit he deserved.
    C He wasted a lot of money.
    D He was unsuccessful.

 / 5

Section Four — Comprehension

Assessment Test 1

The rest of this book contains eight assessment tests, which get progressively harder.

Allow 25 minutes to do each test and work as quickly and as carefully as you can.

If you want to attempt each test more than once, you will need to print **multiple-choice answer sheets** for these questions from our website — go to cgpbooks.co.uk/11plus/answer-sheets or scan the QR code on the right. If you'd prefer to answer them in standard write-in format, just follow the instructions in the question.

Answer Sheets

Read this passage carefully and answer the questions that follow.

Pet Rocks

Have you ever wanted a pet, but been put off by the work needed to take care of it? In 1975, one entrepreneur set about trying to find a solution to this problem. This individual was Gary Dahl, an advertising executive from California, who came up with the unique idea of keeping rocks as pets.

Dahl decided that a rock was an ideal pet because it didn't need feeding, walking or bathing, and
5 there weren't any expensive vet bills to worry about. Certain that Pet Rocks could make his fortune, Dahl started to sell his Rocks to the public.

Over the next year, Dahl sold more than a million Pet Rocks at $3.95 each. Each Rock came with a carrying case complete with air holes and a bed of straw for the Rock's comfort, as well as a thirty-two page instruction manual on how to look after it. These manuals included tips on how to
10 train the Rocks to sit, stay and even roll over (with a bit of help from their owner).

Pet Rocks sold well during the Christmas period, but they were destined to be a fad. Despite Dahl's best efforts they soon became a thing of the past and, after 1975, sales dried up. Fortunately for Dahl, he had already made his fortune.

Nowadays Dahl runs his own advertising company, but he remains an inspiration to many
15 modern inventors. The Pet Rock phenomenon has inspired numerous other creators to think of new crazes that could also sweep the world and make millions of dollars.

Answer these questions about the text that you've just read.
Circle the letter that matches the correct answer.

1. What job did Gary Dahl have before he started selling Pet Rocks?

    A   He ran an advertising company.
    B   He was an entrepreneur.
    C   He worked in marketing.
    D   He worked in advertising.

2. Which of these statements is not true?

    A   Gary Dahl lived in California.
    B   Pet Rocks stopped selling in 1975.
    C   Rocks sold best over Christmas.
    D   The instruction manual said Rocks could be trained to roll over.

/ 2

3. According to the passage, why did Dahl believe that Rocks were the perfect pet?

   1 They are house trained.
   2 They come with an instruction manual.
   3 They don't need exercise.
   4 They don't need veterinary treatment.
   5 They only need bathing once a week.

   A 1 and 2
   B 2 and 3
   C 3 and 4
   D 4 and 5

4. According to the passage, which of these wasn't mentioned in the instruction manual?

   A How to teach the Rock to sit.
   B How to care for your Rock.
   C How to teach the Rock to stay.
   D How to make a bed of straw for your Rock.

5. When were Pet Rocks most successful?

   A December 1975
   B The beginning of 1975
   C After 1975
   D Christmas 1976

6. Why did Pet Rocks stop selling?

   A Dahl ran out of rocks.
   B They were old-fashioned.
   C People lost interest in them.
   D They were too expensive.

7. Why is Gary Dahl inspiring?

   A He runs his own advertising company.
   B He invented the perfect pet.
   C He is rich.
   D He showed that anyone can be successful with the right idea.

/ 5

Carry on to the next question → →

8. What is meant by the word "unique" (line 3)?

    A Unusual
    B Profitable
    C Original
    D Disastrous

9. What is meant by the word "fad" (line 11)?

    A Christmas gift
    B Short-lived trend
    C Bad idea
    D Top-seller

10. Explain the meaning of the phrase "sales dried up" (line 12) as it is used in the passage.

    A People stopped buying Pet Rocks.
    B Pet Rocks stopped being profitable.
    C Pet Rocks were hard to find in the shops.
    D Shops stopped stocking Pet Rocks.

11. Why do you think Pet Rocks sold well at Christmas?

    A People wanted to have a pet over the holiday.
    B People had more time for shopping during the holiday.
    C They made good Christmas decorations.
    D People gave them as gifts.

12. What is meant by the phrase "sweep the world" (line 16)?

    A Take over the planet
    B Clean up the Earth
    C Be popular in many countries
    D Be bought by everyone in the world

/ 5

Find the word that means the opposite, or nearly the opposite, of the word on the left.

Example: big   more   large   <u>little</u>   less

13. **sunrise**   dark   dawn   night   sunset

14. **heavy**   light   huge   dense   tiny

15. **boy**   child   male   girl   old

16. **introduction**   secret   conclusion   origin   late

17. **summer**   month   cold   harvest   winter

18. **never**   when   always   occasionally   often

19. **build**   demolish   apart   restore   construct

20. **safe**   danger   tough   guarded   risky

/ 8

Complete the word on the right so that it means the same, or nearly the same, as the word on the left.

Example: correct   r i g h t

21. **pointy**   s ☐ a r ☐

22. **fast**   h ☐ ☐ t ☐

23. **slim**   s ☐ e ☐ d ☐ r

24. **tired**   s ☐ ☐ ☐ p y

25. **late**   d e ☐ a ☐ e d

26. **middle**   c e ☐ ☐ ☐ e

27. **clever**   b ☐ ☐ i ☐ y

28. **hurt**   i n ☐ ☐ ☐ e

/ 8

Carry on to the next question → →

Fill in the missing letters to complete the words in the following passage.

29.   It was starting to get dark as Ashok and Ben left [s][c][ ][ ][ ][ ][l].

30. They had [s][ ][ ][ ][e][d] late for hockey practice, and then Ben

31. had taken ages to get [c][ ][a][ ][g][e][ ].

32.   Ashok's aunt and [u][ ][ ][ ][e] were coming round for dinner

33. that evening, so he knew he had to get [h][ ][ ][ ][e] quickly.

34.   The boys jogged across the playing [f][ ][ ][ ][ ][d], chatting about

35. the tournament they were due to [c][ ][ ][ ][e][t][e] in on Saturday.

36.   "Come on," said Ben [s][u][d][ ][ ][ ][ ][y], "let's take the short cut

37. past the old warehouse. We'll be home in no [ ][ ][m][e]."

38.   As the boys rounded the [c][o][ ][ ][e][ ] of the warehouse,

39. they noticed a [s][ ][ ][a][ ][g][e] glow coming from one

40. of the [l][a][r][ ][ ][ ] industrial bins.

41.   The lid of the bin was propped [ ][p][e][ ], and as they drew

42. closer they saw what [ ][o][o][ ][ ][d] like a huge egg,

43. half [w][r][ ][ ][ ][e][d] in an old sack, sticking out of the bin.

44. The eerie glow was [c][o][ ][ ][ ][g] from the egg.

/ 16

Three of the words in each list are linked. Mark the word that is not related to these three.

Example: pen   pencil   <u>card</u>   crayon

45. big   huge   mini   gigantic

46. cat   dog   hamster   badger

47. nose   finger   eye   mouth

48. earring   scarf   necklace   bracelet

49. apple   carrot   cabbage   cauliflower

50. work   sing   shout   chat

/ 6

Find the word that means the same, or nearly the same, as the word on the left.

Example: **fantastic**   <u>wonderful</u>   awful   acceptable   expected

51. **alone**   lonely   pathetic   solo   unhappy

52. **wet**   cold   arid   sticky   damp

53. **small**   minuscule   microscope   less   subordinate

54. **happy**   morose   calm   joyous   virtuous

55. **run**   walk   sprint   pace   bounce

56. **draw**   paint   sketch   book   scribble

/ 6

Total   / 56

End of Test

Assessment Test 1

Assessment Test 2

Allow 25 minutes to do this test and work as quickly and as carefully as you can.

You can print **multiple-choice answer sheets** for these questions from our website — go to cgpbooks.co.uk/11plus/answer-sheets or scan the QR code on the right. If you'd prefer to answer them in standard write-in format, just follow the instructions in the question.

Answer Sheets

Read this passage carefully and answer the questions that follow.

The Treasure Hunt

Jimmy looked with increasing frustration from the card in his clammy hand to his friends' bewildered faces. He read the clue aloud, for what felt like the hundredth time:

> "Head west to find the final clue,
> If you cooperate you won't feel blue,

5
> No fowl play, be fair and right,
> And the treasure could be yours tonight."

"We may as well accept defeat in this treasure hunt, Jimmy," whispered Felicity.

Jimmy felt a wave of disappointment crash over him. It was the final evening of Park Hill School's annual camping trip, taking place as usual in the woods surrounding Westbury Farm, and winning the

10 treasure hunt with his best friends would be the perfect way to end the weekend. Jimmy had loved every minute of it: the nature walks, building dens, listening to ghost stories around the campfire and, above all, sleeping outdoors, listening to the strange rustlings of the countryside at night.

Up until this point, they had managed to work out each clue quite swiftly and only Freddie Farley's team was keeping up with them. Freddie, the school football captain, was infamous for being a bad

15 loser and wasn't above using underhand tactics to try to win. Jimmy suspected Freddie was responsible for their broken compass and missing map.

"We are not giving up," said Jimmy, weakly.

"Perhaps 'west' means 'Westbury Farm'?" suggested Felicity, tentatively.

Jimmy's team turned as one to look at the farm. It seemed as though 'coop' and 'fowl' might

20 unravel this maddening mystery.

Answer these questions about the text that you've just read.
Circle the letter that matches the correct answer.

1. Why were Jimmy's friends "bewildered" (line 2)?

   A They were lost in the woods.
   B They were finding the treasure hunt difficult.
   C They did not understand why Jimmy wanted to win.
   D They were confused by the clue.

2. Why did Jimmy feel as though he had read the clue a hundred times?

   A He had already read it 99 times.
   B He was finding the clue hard to read.
   C He had read the clue lots of times, but his team could not solve it.
   D He had read the clue lots of times, but his team were not interested.

/ 2

3. Why did Jimmy speak "weakly" (line 17)?

    A He had lost his voice because he had been talking so much.
    B He did not really believe what he was saying.
    C He was speaking quietly so Freddie wouldn't overhear.
    D He was tired, so he couldn't speak loudly.

4. How often did the school camping trip take place?

    A Once a month
    B Every six months
    C Once a year
    D The text doesn't say

5. Which of the following activities is not mentioned in the text?

    A Building campfires
    B Sleeping outdoors
    C Building dens
    D Listening to ghost stories

6. Why was Freddie "infamous" (line 14)?

    A He was the school football captain.
    B He was using underhand tactics.
    C He couldn't stand it if he didn't win.
    D He had broken Jimmy's team's compass and taken their map.

7. How do you think Jimmy's team feels in lines 19-20?

    A Confused
    B Hopeful
    C Confident
    D Thoughtful

/ 5

Carry on to the next question → →

8. What is meant by the word "frustration" (line 1)?

    A Annoyance
    B Disappointment
    C Worry
    D Shame

9. What is meant by the word "underhand" (line 15)?

    A Tricky
    B Clever
    C Dishonest
    D Secret

10. What is meant by the word "tentatively" (line 18)?

    A Quietly
    B Slowly
    C Hopefully
    D Uncertainly

11. Why do you think the team "turned as one" (line 19)?

    A They heard a noise from the farm.
    B Felicity told them to look at the farm.
    C They all worked out the clue at the same time.
    D They had decided to ask for help at the farm.

12. What is meant by the phrase "you won't feel blue" (line 4)?

    A You won't get lost in the dark.
    B You won't be unhappy.
    C You won't be bored.
    D You will win the treasure hunt.

/ 5

Find the word that means the same, or nearly the same, as the word on the left.

Example: **fantastic** <u>wonderful</u> awful acceptable expected

13. **beach** wave cliff shore holiday

14. **gem** ring rock gold jewel

15. **coat** suit jacket scarf cape

16. **grin** smirk glower frown laugh

17. **storm** tempest frost blowy rain

18. **copy** photograph act imitate tease

19. **joke** prank laugh humour game

20. **ready** strong poise unripe prepared

21. **weak** robust feeble debilitate small

22. **decrease** less rise submerge reduce

/ 10

Find the word that means the opposite, or nearly the opposite, of the word on the left.

Example: **big** more large <u>little</u> less

23. **far** away front beyond near

24. **start** wait try cease here

25. **weep** frown happy sadness giggle

26. **short** slim plump young gangling

27. **speak** teach listen read write

28. **appear** seem present vanish dissolve

29. **healthy** flimsy virus sane diseased

30. **fresh** breezy stale stench original

31. **joy** grief mourn sad goodness

32. **lie** sleep stretch fall stand

/ 10

Carry on to the next question → →

Circle the letters which correspond to the correct words to complete the passage below.

33. **A** easy
Trudy had thought it would be **B** strange to make a campfire.
C warm

34. **A** wanted
Earlier, she had **B** shared a pile of sticks which she had
C collected

35. **A** from
arranged **B** for a wigwam shape. But they must have
C into

36. **A** they
been damp because **B** them refused to catch fire.
C those

37. **A** first
Crossing her fingers, Trudy struck her **B** last match
C only

38. **A** within
and held it gently **B** against the smallest twigs.
C away

39. **A** unexpected
For a moment **B** everything happened. Then Trudy
C nothing

40. **A** rising
saw a plume of smoke **B** burning from one corner.
C falling

41. **A** all
Quickly, she added **B** most twigs to the pile. Suddenly
C more

42. **A** became
the flames caught hold and the pile of sticks **B** becomes
C become

43. **A** snarling
a cheerful, **B** crackling blaze. Trudy grinned and held her
C howling

44. **A** of
chilly hands out towards the warm glow **B** off her fire.
C with

/ 12

In each question below, the words can be rearranged to form a sentence. One word doesn't fit in the sentence. Underline the word that doesn't fit.

Example: dog my long <u>mud</u> walks likes

45. escaped all the egg chickens have

46. hard camping mountains work climbing is very

47. we birthday to that went last year restaurant

48. today Kell is win in the competing marathon

49. I too so tired to my was bedroom clean

50. rug a fort of pillows built out Sasha

/ 6

Complete the word on the right so that it means the opposite, or nearly the opposite, of the word on the left.

Example: dark l i g h t

51. **apart** t ☐ ☐ e t ☐ ☐ r

52. **top** b ☐ ☐ e

53. **son** d ☐ ☐ ☐ ☐ t e r

54. **late** ☐ ☐ ☐ l y

55. **kind** c ☐ ☐ ☐ l

56. **hill** ☐ ☐ ☐ ☐ e y

/ 6

Total / 56

End of Test

Assessment Test 2

Assessment Test 3

Allow 25 minutes to do this test and work as quickly and as carefully as you can.

You can print **multiple-choice answer sheets** for these questions from our website — go to cgpbooks.co.uk/11plus/answer-sheets or scan the QR code on the right. If you'd prefer to answer them in standard write-in format, just follow the instructions in the question.

Answer Sheets

> Read this poem carefully and answer the questions that follow.

An extract from 'The Spider and the Fly'

"Will you walk into my parlour?" said the spider to the fly;
" 'Tis the prettiest little parlour that ever you did spy.
The way into my parlour is up a winding stair,
And I have many curious things to show when you are there."
5 "Oh no, no," said the little fly, "to ask me is in vain,
For who goes up your winding stair can ne'er come down again."

"I'm sure you must be weary, dear, with soaring up so high.
Will you rest upon my little bed?" said the spider to the fly.
"There are pretty curtains drawn around; the sheets are fine and thin,
10 And if you like to rest awhile, I'll snugly tuck you in!"
"Oh no, no," said the little fly, "for I've often heard it said,
They never, never wake again who sleep upon your bed!"

"Sweet creature!" said the spider, "you're witty and you're wise;
How handsome are your gauzy wings; how brilliant are your eyes!
15 I have a little looking-glass upon my parlour shelf;
If you'll step in one moment, dear, you shall behold yourself."
"I thank you, gentle sir," she said, "for what you're pleased to say,
And, bidding you good morning now, I'll call another day."

by Mary Howitt

> Answer these questions about the text that you've just read.
> Circle the letter that matches the correct answer.

1. In the first verse, how does the spider try to get the fly into his parlour?

    A By tempting the fly
    B By flattering the fly
    C By threatening the fly
    D By teasing the fly

2. Which of the following does the spider claim to have in his parlour?

    A A bed with a warm quilt
    B Interesting objects
    C A winding staircase
    D Glass ornaments

/ 2

3. Why does the fly turn down the spider's offer?

   A She doesn't want to climb the staircase.
   B She is not interested in seeing the spider's parlour.
   C She would rather soar up high in the sky.
   D She thinks that she would never escape from the parlour.

4. Why does the spider say that the fly might need to lie on the bed?

   A She will be tired from walking up the stairs.
   B The bed is very comfortable.
   C She will need to rest after looking at the curious things.
   D She is tired from all her flying.

5. How would you describe the fly's attitude towards the spider?

   A Curious
   B Distrustful
   C Grateful
   D Angry

6. In the third verse, what does the spider promise to show the fly?

   A What she looks like
   B A looking-glass
   C The parlour shelf
   D A pair of spectacles

7. The language used by the spider in the third verse could best be described as:

   A polite.
   B kind.
   C flattering.
   D genuine.

/ 5

Carry on to the next question → →

8. What is meant by the word "gauzy" (line 14)?

    A Opaque and valuable
    B Tiny and fragile
    C Thin and transparent
    D Bright and reflective

9. What is meant by the word "behold" (line 16)?

    A Understand
    B View
    C Grasp
    D Approve

10. What is meant by the word "witty" (line 13)?

    A friendly
    B amusing
    C beautiful
    D joyful

11. How do you think the spider feels at the end of the third verse?

    A Jealous, because the fly is so beautiful.
    B Relieved, because he wanted the fly to leave.
    C Disappointed, because the fly has gone.
    D Lonely, because he enjoyed the fly's company.

12. What is meant by the phrase "to ask me is in vain" (line 5)?

    A Asking me shows how big-headed you are.
    B Don't ask me, because I'm big-headed.
    C I'm always being asked into people's homes.
    D There is no point in asking me.

/ 5

Find the word that means the opposite, or nearly the opposite, of the word on the left.

Example: **big**   more   large   <u>little</u>   less

13. **awake**   tired   sleeping   conscious   numb

14. **spiky**   prickly   curve   round   blunt

15. **attic**   stairs   floor   cellar   loft

16. **exit**   into   leave   enter   go

17. **inside**   exterior   away   central   airy

18. **find**   fail   drain   vanish   lose

19. **bad**   tolerant   acceptable   saintly   proper

20. **hungry**   gorge   satisfied   fat   consumed

21. **success**   grief   problem   fallacy   failure

22. **limited**   endless   finite   many   narrow

/ 10

Complete the word on the right so that it means the opposite, or nearly the opposite, of the word on the left.

Example: dark    l i g h t

23. **evening**   m ☐ ☐ n ☐ ☐ g

24. **odd**   ☐ ☐ e ☐

25. **curse**   b ☐ ☐ ☐ s

26. **silly**   s ☐ n s ☐ ☐ ☐ e

27. **admit**   d ☐ ☐ y

28. **go**   ☐ ☐ m ☐

/ 6

Carry on to the next question → →

Assessment Test 3

Fill in the missing letters to complete the words in the following passage.

29. Whenever we go for a w___ in the woods,

30. Dad likes to l e____ r e us on the surroundings.

31. Once it was on the way leaves turn b____n in autumn,

32. and another time we estimated the h___g__t and age of the biggest trees.

33. When he declared, "We're __o__n__ to Brook Valley today,"

34. Mita and I g r____e d: Brook Valley was by far the furthest trail from the car park!

35. While Dad was trying to work out __h__r__ we were on the map,

36. Mita and I deliberately dashed off in the __p__o s__t e direction,

37. racing each __t____r to be first up the hill.

38. We could hear Dad's shouts getting __a i____t__r in the distance

39. and we knew he'd be annoyed, but we didn't __a r__ — we were

40. determined that __o d____ was going to be fun!

/ 12

Mark the word outside the brackets that has a similar meaning to the words in both sets of brackets.

Example: (charge fee)   (sunny bright)   summer   cost   <u>fine</u>

41. (alter   adjust)   (coins   money)   adapt   fee   change

42. (knock   tap)   (hip-hop   urban)   rap   music   throw

43. (sack   dismiss)   (blaze   flames)   expel   bring   fire

44. (look   observe)   (clock   timer)   watch   time   view

45. (jump   leap)   (cellar   safe)   box   vault   bound

46. (feathers   fluff)   (below   under)   down   fuzz   beneath

/ 6

Find the word that means the same, or nearly the same, as the word on the left.

Example: **fantastic**   <u>wonderful</u>   awful   acceptable   expected

47. **curious**   interested   informed   look   customary

48. **tired**   boring   yawn   drowsy   asleep

49. **cup**   plate   jug   fork   goblet

50. **boring**   bizarre   drag   tedious   usual

51. **chore**   struggle   task   sweat   lazy

52. **worry**   thought   remember   concern   horror

53. **ill**   rotten   feeble   cold   ailing

54. **tall**   huge   towering   stunted   steep

55. **own**   possess   mine   maintain   control

56. **baby**   youth   child   infant   boy

/ 10

Total   / 56

End of Test

Assessment Test 3

Assessment Test 4

Allow 25 minutes to do this test and work as quickly and as carefully as you can.

You can print **multiple-choice answer sheets** for these questions from our website — go to cgpbooks.co.uk/11plus/answer-sheets or scan the QR code on the right. If you'd prefer to answer them in standard write-in format, just follow the instructions in the question.

Answer
Sheets

Read this passage carefully and answer the questions that follow.

Adapted from 'The Wind in the Willows'

The afternoon sun was getting low as the Rat sculled gently homewards in a dreamy mood, not paying much attention to Mole. But the Mole was very full of lunch, and self-satisfaction, and pride, and already quite at home in a boat (so he thought) and was getting a bit restless: and presently he said, "Ratty! Please, *I* want to row, now!"

5   The Rat shook his head with a smile. "Not yet, my young friend, wait till you've had a few lessons. It's not so easy as it looks."

The Mole was quiet for a minute or two. But he began to feel more and more jealous of Rat, sculling so strongly and so easily along, and his pride began to whisper that he could do it every bit as well. He jumped up and seized the sculls, so suddenly, that the Rat, who was gazing out over

10   the water, was taken by surprise and fell backwards off his seat with his legs in the air, while the triumphant Mole took his place and grabbed the sculls with entire confidence.

"Stop it!" cried the Rat. "You can't do it! You'll have us over!"

The Mole flung his sculls back with a flourish, and made a great dig at the water. He missed the surface altogether, his legs flew up above his head, and he found himself lying on top of the prostrate

15   Rat. Greatly alarmed, he made a grab at the side of the boat, and the next moment – sploosh!

Over went the boat, and he found himself struggling in the river.

by Kenneth Grahame

Answer these questions about the text that you've just read.
Circle the letter that matches the correct answer.

1.   At what time of the day were Mole and Rat rowing?

    A   Late morning
    B   Early afternoon
    C   Late afternoon
    D   Late evening

2.   Which statement about Mole is not true?

    A   He was in a dreamy mood.
    B   He was impatient.
    C   He had eaten lots.
    D   He envied Rat.

/ 2

3.   Why did Rat not allow Mole to row?

    A   It was Rat's boat and he didn't want to share.
    B   They were nearly home.
    C   He thought Mole needed to practise first.
    D   He thought Mole was not a good rower.

4.   Why was Mole jealous of Rat?

    A   Rat was not paying him any attention.
    B   Rat was a very skilful rower.
    C   Rat would not let him row.
    D   Rat had a boat.

5.   What happened to Rat when Mole grabbed the sculls?

    A   He fell backwards into the boat.
    B   He fell on top of Mole.
    C   He fell into the water.
    D   He was knocked over by a scull.

6.   Once Mole had the sculls, which one of the following things did not happen?

    A   Rat shouted at Mole.
    B   Mole tried to show off with the sculls.
    C   Mole lost his balance and fell onto Rat.
    D   Mole accidentally hit Rat with the sculls.

7.   Which adjective best describes Mole in lines 9-11?

    A   Reckless
    B   Jealous
    C   Brave
    D   Impressive

/ 5

Carry on to the next question → →

8. Mole felt "at home in a boat" (line 3). What does this expression mean?

    A   He felt lazy.
    B   He felt proud.
    C   He felt comfortable.
    D   He felt welcome.

9. What is meant by the word "triumphant" (line 11)?

    A   Strong
    B   Victorious
    C   Boastful
    D   Lucky

10. What is meant by the word "alarmed" (line 15)?

    A   Concerned
    B   Noisy
    C   Upset
    D   Panicked

11. What is meant by the word "prostrate" (line 14)?

    A   Lying down flat
    B   Badly injured
    C   Extremely angry
    D   Helpless with laughter

12. What is meant by the phrase "his pride began to whisper" (line 8)?

    A   He started to talk quietly.
    B   He felt the need to prove himself.
    C   He started to feel ashamed.
    D   He felt pleased with his voice.

/ 5

Three of the words in each list are linked. Mark the word that is not related to these three.

Example: pen   pencil   <u>card</u>   crayon

13. kitchen   garage   bedroom   study

14. cup   mug   plate   beaker

15. lamb   fawn   sow   foal

16. hail   cloud   rain   snow

17. baby   boy   lady   child

18. grimace   peer   scowl   frown

/ 6

Complete the word on the right so that it means the same, or nearly the same, as the word on the left.

Example: correct [r][i][g][h][t]

19. **start** [ ][e][ ][ ][n]

20. **away** [ ][b][s][ ][ ][t]

21. **decrease** [d][ ][c][ ][ ][ ][e]

22. **mean** [s][t][ ][ ][ ][y]

23. **fair** [j][ ][ ][ ]

24. **tidy** [ ][e][a][ ]

25. **tiny** [ ][i][ ][u][ ][ ]

26. **clear** [o][ ][v][ ][ ][ ][s]

/ 8

Carry on to the next question → →

Circle the letters which correspond to the correct words to complete the passage below.

27. **A** difficult
Hester crept through the   **B** dense   undergrowth, signalling to Benito, her cameraman, to
C friendly

28. **A** remain   29. **A** opportunities
B remaining silent. To Hester, the forest was a treasure chest of filming   **B** things   ;
C remains   **C** problems

30. **A** will
she just hoped that today   **B** can   be a good day. She cursed softly as thorny vines gleefully
C would

31. **A** by   32. **A** Parting
tangled themselves   **B** in   her mop of curly blonde hair.   **B** Sharing the emerald-green
C about   **C** Joining

33. **A** near
ferns, Hester gasped. A few metres   **B** far   from her was a whole family of chimps. She couldn't
C away

34. **A** luck
believe her   **B** joy   .
C job

35. **A** who   36. **A** face
Making sure   **B** that   Benito was recording, she turned breathlessly to   **B** look the camera.
C when   **C** film

37. **A** yelled
"This is a rare sight," she   **B** cried   quietly to the camera. "As you can see, the large male is
C said

38. **A** mushy   39. **A** Besides
cracking the   **B** hard   outer shells of nuts.   **B** Despite   , the female is grooming her infant,
C tasty   **C** Meanwhile

cradling him carefully in her hands."

40. **A** closed
As Hester watched, the young chimp   **B** close   its eyes and let its head fall back against its
C closes

41. **A** teeth
mother. Its   **B** mouth was curved into a contented smile, and for a moment the chimp reminded
C chin

42. **A** was
Hester of her own son when he   **B** were a baby.
C is

/ 16

Find the word that means the opposite, or nearly the opposite, of the word on the left.

Example: **big**   more   large   <u>little</u>   less

43. **lose**   trophy   medal   second   triumph

44. **above**   beside   inside   down   beneath

45. **lend**   offer   borrow   deliver   bring

46. **selfish**   pensive   popular   generous   tedious

47. **modern**   museum   antique   relic   remains

48. **misplace**   obtain   require   gain   retrieve

/ 6

Find the word that means the same, or nearly the same, as the word on the left.

Example: **fantastic**   <u>wonderful</u>   awful   acceptable   expected

49. **cook**   melt   burn   chef   servant

50. **rest**   idle   relax   silence   comfort

51. **waste**   stench   increase   rotten   rubbish

52. **box**   kick   hurt   trunk   bin

53. **relation**   friend   associate   kin   familiar

54. **dress**   gown   cloak   skirt   wardrobe

55. **tasty**   scrumptious   pungent   wholesome   insipid

56. **hate**   ambivalent   detest   averse   revolt

/ 8

Total   / 56

End of Test

Assessment Test 4

Assessment Test 5

Allow 25 minutes to do this test and work as quickly and as carefully as you can.

You can print **multiple-choice answer sheets** for these questions from our website — go to cgpbooks.co.uk/11plus/answer-sheets or scan the QR code on the right. If you'd prefer to answer them in standard write-in format, just follow the instructions in the question.

Answer Sheets

Read this passage carefully and answer the questions that follow.

The Bizarre Bazaar

Michael stood in the freezing downpour, staring between the sodden canvas drapes of a market stall at a beautiful miniature elephant carved from ivory. He stepped under the deserted awning and picked up the ornament.

Immediately, his body tingled as if an electric current was flowing through him and he felt a wave
5   of dizziness, forcing his eyes shut.

He opened his eyes to see a huge elephant charging towards him, and leapt aside just in time. A much smaller elephant ran past, followed by two men carrying rifles. The large elephant charged onwards, unaware that its baby had become entangled in a clump of scrub. The baby elephant stood petrified as the hunters approached.
10   "There's no point shooting the baby," said the shorter of the men. "It doesn't have tusks. No tusks means no ivory to sell."

"True," said his taller companion. "Let's go after the adult elephant."

"No, Kevin! Any second now, she'll notice her baby isn't with her. All we have to do is wait." He smirked and held up his gun.
15   Michael watched, horrified, as the adult elephant stopped and turned. The hunters raised their rifles. He ran towards them, waving his arms and yelling loudly. The terrified baby elephant thrashed wildly and freed itself from the scrub and both elephants charged off into the distance. The hunters stared in amazement.

The air shimmered and, seconds later, Michael was back in the bazaar. His heart was pounding
20   and he was disorientated. He looked down and cried out when he saw his empty hands; the ivory ornament had disappeared. Michael was bewildered for a moment and then it hit him: by saving the elephant he had prevented the ornament ever being made.

Answer these questions about the text that you've just read.
Circle the letter that matches the correct answer.

1.   Which of the following statements is not true?

   A   Michael saw the ornament on a market stall.
   B   Michael was the only customer at the stall.
   C   It was a hot summer's day.
   D   The ornament was carved from elephant tusks.

/ 1

2. Why did the elephant charge towards Michael?

    A It wanted to hurt him.
    B It thought he was going to hurt the young elephant.
    C It was running after its baby.
    D It was fleeing from the hunters.

3. Why did the hunters decide to spare the young elephant?

    A They were kind-hearted.
    B It was illegal to shoot young elephants.
    C They didn't want to anger the adult elephant.
    D They would not make any money by killing it.

4. Why was Michael "horrified" (line 15)?

    A He was afraid the hunter would shoot him.
    B He was afraid the elephant would hurt him.
    C He was afraid the hunters would shoot the adult elephant.
    D He was afraid the hunters would shoot the baby elephant.

5. How do you think Michael felt in line 20?

    A Exhausted
    B Confused
    C Excited
    D Sick

6. What does Michael realise at the end of the story?

    A He has mislaid the ornament.
    B He has changed history.
    C He imagined the ornament.
    D His adventure was just a dream.

7. Which of the following facts is not given in the story?

    A The name of the shorter hunter.
    B The name of the main character.
    C The substance the ornament was made from.
    D The reason the men were hunting the elephant.

8. What is meant by the word "thrashed" (line 16)?

    A Flailed
    B Jumped
    C Spun
    D Stamped

/ 7

Carry on to the next question → →

> Find the word that means the opposite, or nearly the opposite, of the word on the left.
>
> **Example:** **big**   more   large   <u>little</u>   less

9. **teacher**   headmaster   student   mentor   amateur

10. **right**   fault   proper   left   imprecise

11. **short**   lengthy   stretch   distant   soon

12. **young**   recent   experienced   develop   ancient

13. **jolly**   sullen   stubborn   annoying   tired

14. **cheap**   posh   reasonable   overpriced   exquisite

15. **release**   freedom   deliver   condemn   imprison

16. **see-through**   dark   opaque   foggy   clear

17. **brittle**   rigid   pliable   bend   shatter

18. **patient**   tolerant   willing   greedy   doctor

/ 10

> Complete the word on the right so that it means the opposite, or nearly the opposite, of the word on the left.
>
> **Example: dark**   [l][i][g][h][t]

19. **thin**   [t][ ][ ][c][ ]

20. **loose**   [ ][i][ ][h][ ]

21. **war**   [ ][e][ ][c][ ]

22. **functional**   [ ][s][e][l][ ][ ][s]

23. **over**   [ ][e][ ][o][ ]

24. **rude**   [c][ ][ ][ ][l]

25. **junior**   [ ][ ][p][e][r][i][ ][r]

26. **cry**   [c][ ][ ][ ][k][ ][e]

27. **grow**   [ ][ ][r][i][ ][ ]

28. **low**   [l][ ][ ][ ][y]

/ 10

Read the information carefully and answer the questions that follow.

The Big Race

Thursday dawned bright and sunny, with wisps of white cloud chasing one another across a sapphire sky. On the playing field, the grass had been newly mown and the tracks freshly marked with white paint. Amita stood on the bank overlooking the field and inhaled deeply. She loved Sports Day, and this year she knew she could beat her arch-rival, Gabby Steele, in the egg-and-spoon race.

Gradually the rest of Amita's team, all clad in bright yellow T-shirts, gathered around her to survey the field of battle. To her left she could see Dean pointing out someone in the crowd to Sara and Chandani, while on her right Josh, Rani and Simon stood together in silent comradeship.

The day passed in a blur of events. Sara won the sack race, while Dean and Rani were narrowly beaten by Peter and Ben, from Gabby's team, in the three-legged race. With only the egg-and-spoon race to go, the yellow team were tied for first place with the blue team. It all came down to Amita and Gabby.

A hush fell upon the crowd as five figures separated themselves from their blocks of colour, collected their eggs and spoons, and positioned themselves on the start line. A crack of the starter's pistol and they were off! Julia, from the orange team, took an early lead, but Paul, from the green team, caught her up and they finished at the same time. Gabby finished two seconds before Paul, but skidded and finished one second behind Will, from the red team. Amita beat Julia by four seconds.

Answer these questions about the text that you've just read.
Circle the letter that matches the correct answer.

29. Which of these statements must be true?

    A   Gabby came last in the egg-and-spoon race.
    B   Paul finished before Will.
    C   Amita and Will tied for first place.
    D   Julia finished after Will.

30. Which of these statements cannot be true?

    A   The blue team won the three-legged race.
    B   The blue team were the overall winners.
    C   The red team won more races than the green team.
    D   Amita was captain of the yellow team.

31. How do you think Amita feels as she looks across the playing field?

    A   Nervous, because winning means a lot to her.
    B   Proud, because she knows her team will win.
    C   Confident, because she thinks she will do well.
    D   Happy, because she has all her friends around her.

32. Which of these statements cannot be true?

    A   Peter was on the blue team.
    B   During her race, Gabby slipped on some long grass.
    C   It was a warm summer day.
    D   Dean's mum came to support him.

/ 4

Carry on to the next question → →

Fill in the missing letters to complete the words in the following passage

33. The alarm pierced the q ☐ ☐ e t of the fire station.

34. Amanda's body t i ☐ ☐ ☐ e d with excitement;

35. this was the ☐ ☐ ☐ e n t she had been training for!

36. Racing to the ☐ ☐ ☐ r l e t fire engine,

37. Amanda ☐ ☐ l ☐ apprehensive yet confident.

38. The journey was swift and, ☐ f ☐ e ☐ a few minutes,

39. the engine swerved ☐ ☐ ☐ o a car park.

40. Amanda dashed into the b ☐ ☐ z ☐ ☐ g building and heard faint calls for help.

41. Gingerly, she inched along the smoke-filled ☐ o r ☐ ☐ d o ☐.

42. Entering a ☐ e d ☐ ☐ o ☐, she saw a terrified child huddled under the bed.

43. Scooping him up, she smashed the ☐ ☐ n d ☐ ☐

44. and carried him down the ☐ a i ☐ ☐ n ☐ ladder to safety.

/ 12

> Find the word that means the same, or nearly the same, as the word on the left.
>
> **Example:** fantastic   <u>wonderful</u> awful acceptable expected

45. **inspire**   relieve expire motivate attend

46. **wreckage**   cost forget tedium debris

47. **plenty**   poverty sated abundance generous

48. **answer**   repeat react agree reply

49. **chase**   search find pursue hasten

50. **sign**   wave omen proof hinted

51. **swerve**   veer launch trudge leap

52. **choose**   decision preference wish select

53. **piece**   allocate accord segment provide

54. **dull**   gloomy active ache heavy

55. **order**   inquire command advise ask

56. **keep**   held release relieve preserve

/ 12

Total   / 56

End of Test

Assessment Test 5

Assessment Test 6

Allow 25 minutes to do this test and work as quickly and as carefully as you can.

You can print **multiple-choice answer sheets** for these questions from our website — go to cgpbooks.co.uk/11plus/answer-sheets or scan the QR code on the right. If you'd prefer to answer them in standard write-in format, just follow the instructions in the question.

> Read this passage carefully and answer the questions that follow.

Echo and Narcissus

Narcissus was a Greek hunter who was renowned for his beauty. Countless women came to his home town of Thespiae to seduce him, which made Narcissus very arrogant. He rejected all of his admirers, because he thought that none of them were good enough.

Narcissus often hunted for deer in the forests. These forests were full of nymphs: divine creatures
5 who kept the plants, trees and animals alive. One nymph, named Echo, fell in love with Narcissus, but he rejected her as well.

With her heart broken, Echo fled to a secret spring, where she faded away. Nemesis, a powerful goddess, saw how Narcissus had treated Echo, and decided to take revenge.

One day, Nemesis lured Narcissus to the spring where Echo had died. As he approached the
10 water, Narcissus glimpsed an attractive face in the water and, thinking it was a beautiful water spirit, he fell in love with it. He bent down to kiss the spirit, but the water rippled and it vanished.

When the water became still, the spirit returned. Again, Narcissus tried to touch it, but again his efforts were to no avail. When the spirit returned for a third time, Narcissus just gazed intently at the face.

The sun rose and set many times, but still Narcissus stayed by the spring, pining for his love,
15 growing weaker and weaker because he didn't want to leave. Without food or sleep, he rapidly weakened and died. On the bank of the spring where his body had been, a white flower sprouted and blossomed, and this flower bears the name narcissus.

> Answer these questions about the text that you've just read.
> Circle the letter that matches the correct answer.

1. Why did Narcissus reject his admirers?

   A He thought he was better than them.
   B He didn't think that he was good enough for them.
   C He didn't think they were attractive enough.
   D He didn't think they were wealthy enough.

2. According to the passage, what are nymphs?

   A Gods that planted trees.
   B Heavenly beings that tended to the forests.
   C Gardeners that looked after divine creatures.
   D Spirits that created magical forests.

(/ 2)

3. Which of these statements is true?

   A Nemesis was a nymph.
   B Narcissus did not fall in love with Echo.
   C Echo took revenge on Narcissus.
   D Nemesis was rejected by Narcissus.

4. Why do you think Echo ran away to the spring?

   A To look after the trees, plants and animals.
   B She wanted to see Narcissus.
   C She was upset and wanted to be alone.
   D She was meeting Nemesis there.

5. Why did the face Narcissus saw in the water keep disappearing?

   A It was afraid of Narcissus.
   B It did not love Narcissus.
   C It was Echo's ghost.
   D It was a reflection.

6. How long did Narcissus stay by the spring?

   A Weeks
   B Years
   C Decades
   D Forever

7. What do you think this myth is a warning against?

   A Talking to strangers
   B Being too attractive
   C Falling in love
   D Being obsessed with how you look

/ 5

Carry on to the next question → →

8.   What is meant by the word "renowned" (line 1)?

   A   Worshipped
   B   Admired
   C   Cursed
   D   Famous

9.   What is meant by the word "arrogant" (line 2)?

   A   Angry
   B   Confident
   C   Conceited
   D   Courageous

10.   What is meant by the word "lured" (line 9)?

   A   Dragged
   B   Tricked
   C   Enticed
   D   Directed

11.   What does the phrase "to no avail" (line 13) mean?

   A   Without hope
   B   Not successful
   C   An impediment
   D   Badly received

12.   What does the phrase "pining for his love" (line 14) mean?

   A   Wasting away with longing
   B   Burning with love
   C   Grieving for the water spirit
   D   Missing the forest nymphs

/ 5

In each question below, the words can be rearranged to form a sentence. One word doesn't fit in the sentence. Underline the word that doesn't fit.

Example: dog my long <u>mud</u> walks likes

13. am in outside to I play snowflakes going the snow

14. mittens is fluffy hat purple and favourite my

15. home lost track way got very his late Harry and

16. the nest built a out eggs of and moss birds twigs

17. present town Alisha is to buy a birthday going into brother

18. but nothing have play games computer all day sit done you

/ 6

Mark the word outside the brackets that has a similar meaning to the words in both sets of brackets.

Example: (charge fee)   (sunny bright)   summer   cost   <u>fine</u>

19. (holiday voyage)   (fall stumble)   tour   plunge   trip

20. (period time)   (magic incantation) stretch   spell   charm

21. (tiny miniature)   (moment instant)   small   clock   minute

22. (hurried quick)   (abstain diet)   fast   hasty   slim

23. (empty void)   (cave dip)   free   hollow   cavern

24. (shape sculpt)   (decay rot)   mould   whittle   spoil

25. (iron copper)   (steer escort)   metal   lead   guide

26. (bare barren)   (leave abandon)   desert   forsake   arid

27. (basin washbowl)   (descend plummet)   bath   plunge   sink

28. (perfume aroma)   (anger annoy)   scent   infuriate incense

/ 10

Carry on to the next question → →

Assessment Test 6

Fill in the missing letters to complete the words in the following passage.

29. Jack was t h ☐ ☐ ☐ l l ☐ to get a metal detector for his birthday.

30. He spent the ☐ ☐ ☐ l e day planning his first outing.

31. He w ☐ ☐ l ☐ pack a picnic, take the bus to the beach

32. and find some b ☐ ☐ ☐ ☐ d treasure!

33. The next day he got up at ☐ a w ☐ to put his plan into action.

34. Everything went smoothly ☐ n ☐ i ☐ he opened his bag

35. and realised something ☐ ☐ f ☐ l —

36. he had forgotten to bring the b a ☐ ☐ e r ☐ pack!

37. All he could do was ☐ a ☐ his picnic,

38. paddle in the sea and wait for the bus ☐ ☐ m ☐.

39. But he vowed to come ☐ ☐ ☐ k the following day,

40. this time with everything he n ☐ ☐ ☐ e ☐.

/ 12

Complete the word on the right so that it means the same, or nearly the same, as the word on the left.

Example: correct r i g h t

41. **spite** ☐ ☐ l ☐ c e

42. **evil** w i ☐ ☐ ☐ ☐

43. **near** c ☐ ☐ ☐ e

44. **compliment** p ☐ ☐ i ☐ e

45. **worried** ☐ ☐ x i ☐ ☐ s

46. **agree** c o ☐ ☐ ☐ ☐ t

/ 6

Find the word that means the opposite, or nearly the opposite, of the word on the left.

Example: **big** more large <u>little</u> less

47. **alone** group consecutive separate together

48. **early** punctual lazy keen overdue

49. **smile** miserable sulk frown sneer

50. **still** again also windy although

51. **rise** emerge sleep descend expose

52. **immense** vast petty microscopic narrow

53. **full** abandoned replete hunger famished

54. **admire** crave bore despise avert

55. **smooth** monotonous crumbled level wrinkled

56. **exact** approximate unknown specific doubtful

/ 10

Total / 56

End of Test

Assessment Test 6

Assessment Test 7

Allow 25 minutes to do this test and work as quickly and as carefully as you can.

You can print **multiple-choice answer sheets** for these questions from our website — go to cgpbooks.co.uk/11plus/answer-sheets or scan the QR code on the right. If you'd prefer to answer them in standard write-in format, just follow the instructions in the question.

Answer
Sheets

> Read this passage carefully and answer the questions that follow.

An extract from 'The Jungle Book'

"Man!" he snapped. "A man's cub. Look!"

Directly in front of him, holding on by a low branch, stood a naked brown baby who could just walk, as soft and as dimpled a little atom as ever came to a wolf's cave at night. He looked up into Father Wolf's face and laughed.

5   "Is that a man's cub?" said Mother Wolf. "I have never seen one. Bring it here."

A wolf accustomed to moving his own cubs can, if necessary, mouth an egg without breaking it, and though Father Wolf's jaws closed right on the child's back not a tooth even scratched the skin, as he laid it down among the cubs.

"How little! How naked, and — how bold!" said Mother Wolf, softly. The baby was pushing his

10 way between the cubs to get close to the warm hide. "Ahai! He is taking his meal with the others. And so this is a man's cub. Now, was there ever a wolf that could boast of a man's cub among her children?"

"I have heard now and again of such a thing, but never in our pack or in my time," said Father Wolf. "He is altogether without hair, and I could kill him with a touch of my foot. But see, he looks up

15 and is not afraid."

The moonlight was blocked out of the mouth of the cave, for Shere Khan's great square head and shoulders were thrust into the entrance. Tabaqui, behind him, was squeaking: "My Lord, my Lord, it went in here!"

by Rudyard Kipling

> Answer these questions about the text that you've just read.
> Circle the letter that matches the correct answer.

1.   Why do the wolves call the child a "man's cub" (line 1)?

    A   They know whose baby it is.
    B   A baby wolf is called a "cub".
    C   They are scared of the child.
    D   It does not have any hair.

2.   How does the reader know that the child is not a new-born baby?

    A   The child can walk.
    B   The child can talk.
    C   The child has hair.
    D   The child isn't afraid.

/ 2

3. How does Father Wolf pick the baby up?

    A Roughly
    B Gently
    C Fiercely
    D Carelessly

4. Why does Father Wolf say "I could kill him with a touch of my foot" (line 14)?

    A He is threatening the child because he does not like humans.
    B He is explaining how small and weak the baby is.
    C He wants to frighten the child to make him less bold.
    D He wants to punish the child for eating the cubs' food.

5. Which two of the following are given as reasons for the baby pushing his way in amongst the cubs?

    1 He is afraid of Father Wolf.
    2 He is hiding from Shere Khan.
    3 He is looking for food.
    4 He is trying to get warm.
    5 He wants to go to sleep.

    A 1 and 5
    B 3 and 4
    C 2 and 4
    D 3 and 5

6. Which of the following statements is not true?

    A Mother Wolf is intrigued by the child.
    B Mother and Father Wolf have cubs of their own.
    C Father Wolf discovered the child.
    D Mother Wolf has seen human children before.

7. Who do you think Tabaqui is?

    A Shere Khan's lord
    B Shere Khan's sidekick
    C The owner of the cave
    D A friend of Father Wolf

/ 5

Carry on to the next question → →

8. What does the phrase "accustomed to" (line 6) mean?

   A Unfamiliar with
   B Attempting to
   C Cautious of
   D Used to

9. What is meant by the word "hide" (line 10)?

   A Skin
   B Conceal
   C Shelter
   D Animal

10. What is meant by the word "thrust" (line 17)?

    A Placed
    B Nudged
    C Shoved
    D Located

11. How do you think Mother Wolf feels about the baby pushing between her cubs?

    A Proud, because she doesn't know of any other wolf who has nursed a human child.
    B Angry, because he's pushing her cubs out of the way.
    C Frightened, because she has never seen a human child before.
    D Amused, because he thinks that he's a wolf.

12. What does the phrase "mouth an egg" (line 6) mean?

    A Swallow an egg
    B Suck an egg
    C Steal an egg
    D Carry an egg

/ 5

Circle the letters which correspond to the correct words to complete the passage below.

It came without warning. The day had started cold but

13.
A bright
B chilly
C dull
D cloudy

, the sunlight sharpening

the edges of the trees

14.
A from
B through
C with
D against

the sky. Towards noon, leaden clouds gathered

15.
A merrily
B suddenly
C instantly
D precisely

and with them the first flurries of snow. The wind sprang from

16.
A nowhere
B north
C around
D corners

,

whipping the flakes into a frenzy, and within minutes the countryside

17.
A is
B was
C were
D will be

obscured.

High

18.
A below
B from
C behind
D above

the village, Achak pulled his sister closer in the darkness. When the blizzard

began, they had searched frantically for

19.
A snow
B berries
C shelter
D people

, Alawa clinging to Achak's hand

as he

20.
A dragged
B bullied
C carried
D abandoned

her deeper into the forest where the trees would

21.
A accept
B provide
C deprive
D hinder

some

kind of break against the icy winds and drifting

22.
A breeze
B ice
C storm
D snow

. Almost blinded and half frozen, he

had

23.
A seen
B see
C saw
D seed

it: a dark slash against the white. Exhausted, the two children had

24.
A skipped
B crawled
C looked
D flown

into the temporary protection of the cave. Alawa's tiny body

25.
A shakes
B shaked
C shook
D shaking

violently despite her

furs. Gradually the combined

26.
A chill
B peace
C warmth
D furs

of their bodies stilled the tremors and she fell asleep,

still

27.
A clutching
B clutch
C clutched
D clutches

the bag of herbs they had been collecting in the

28.
A village
B forest
C town
D river

when the

storm started.

/ 16

Carry on to the next question → →

Assessment Test 7

Find the word that means the same, or nearly the same, as the word on the left.

Example: **fantastic**   <u>wonderful</u>   awful   acceptable   expected

29. **ridiculous**   absurd   awful   funny   teased

30. **ask**   claim   need   pry   request

31. **tease**   soothe   laugh   taunt   bother

32. **praise**   value   censure   like   applaud

33. **annoy**   aggravate   inflict   appease   confront

34. **comfort**   lessen   snug   solace   melancholy

35. **push**   pull   yank   strain   press

36. **pamper**   ignore   indulge   oblige   entertain

/ 8

Three of the words in each list are linked. Mark the word that is not related to these three.

Example: pen   pencil   <u>card</u>   crayon

37. lake   pond   stream   reservoir

38. mouse   monitor   stereo   keyboard

39. wellingtons   anorak   parasol   umbrella

40. limerick   hymn   sonnet   haiku

41. Germany   France   Spain   India

42. heart   knee   shoulder   hip

/ 6

71

Complete the word on the right so that it means the same, or nearly the same, as the word on the left.

Example: correct r i g h t

43. **chatty** ☐☐l☐at☐v e

44. **abroad** o v☐☐☐e a☐

45. **angry** ☐l☐☐☐d

46. **winner** v☐c☐o☐

47. **repeat** ☐c h☐

48. **round** ☐i☐c u☐a r

49. **explain** c☐a☐☐f y

50. **first** ☐r☐m☐r y

/ 8

Find the word that means the opposite, or nearly the opposite, of the word on the left.

Example: **big** more large <u>little</u> less

51. **freedom** captive arrest confinement restrained

52. **advance** backward fail hesitate retreat

53. **refuse** trash grant forfeit applaud

54. **accidental** deliberate intent careful balanced

55. **willing** indecisive pliable doubtful stubborn

56. **better** badly inferior minor dubious

/ 6

Assessment Test 8

Allow 25 minutes to do this test and work as quickly and as carefully as you can.

You can print **multiple-choice answer sheets** for these questions from our website — go to cgpbooks.co.uk/11plus/answer-sheets or scan the QR code on the right If you'd prefer to answer them in standard write-in format, just follow the instructions in the question.

Answer
Sheets

> Read this poem carefully and answer the questions that follow.

Adapted from 'Travel'

I should like to rise and go
Where the golden apples grow;—

Where below another sky
Parrot islands anchored lie,
5   And, watched by cockatoos and goats,
Lonely Crusoes building boats;—

Where in sunshine reaching out
Eastern cities, miles about,
Are with mosque and minaret
10 Among sandy gardens set,
And the rich goods from near and far
Hang for sale in the bazaar;—

Where the Great Wall round China goes,
And on one side the desert blows,
15 And with the bell and voice and drum,
Cities on the other hum;—

Where are forests, hot as fire,
Wide as England, tall as a spire,
Where the knotty crocodile
20 Lies and blinks in the Nile,
And the red flamingo flies
Hunting fish before his eyes;—

Where in jungles, near and far,
Man-devouring tigers are,
25 Lying close and giving ear
Lest the hunt be drawing near.

by Robert Louis Stevenson

> Answer these questions about the text that you've just read.
> Circle the letter that matches the correct answer.

1.   What is the poem about?

   A   The poet is describing all the places he has visited.
   B   The poet is imagining the places he would like to visit.
   C   The poet is describing places he would not like to visit.
   D   The poet is persuading people to travel to these places.

2.   What does the poet mean when he says "below another sky" (line 3)?

   A   On a different planet
   B   During better weather
   C   In another country
   D   In a different climate

(/ 2)

3. Which of these statements about the eastern cities is not true?

    A   Their markets sell only local produce.
    B   There are religious buildings in them.
    C   They are very large.
    D   They have sandy gardens.

4. Which of these best describes what the crocodile is doing?

    A   Lying with his eyes closed
    B   Hiding in the water
    C   Watching the fish
    D   Watching the flamingo fly

5. What mood does the poet create in lines 15-16?

    A   Serene
    B   Bustling
    C   Exotic
    D   Carefree

6. Which of these best describes what the tiger is doing?

    A   Hiding from people
    B   Hunting for prey
    C   Waiting to catch people
    D   Lying and listening for hunters

7. Which of these places is not mentioned in the poem?

    A   Deserted cities
    B   Expansive forests
    C   Exotic orchards
    D   Colourful markets

8. What is meant by the word "devouring" (line 24)?

    A   Threatening
    B   Roaring
    C   Eating
    D   Hunting

/ 6

Carry on to the next question → →

Assessment Test 8

74

> Circle the letters which correspond to the correct words to complete the passage below.

The World Conker Championships

9. **A** begin
B began
C begun
D begins

in 1965, when a small group of friends from

Ashton in Northamptonshire were unable to organise a fishing trip

10. **A** because
B due to
C now
D considering

the weather

was so bad. At a loss for a fun way to

11. **A** waste
B consume
C relive
D spend

their day, they decided to play conkers.

Since then, the

12. **A** conker
B event
C hobby
D fun

has grown considerably. In 2004, the Championships attracted

more than five hundred participants and huge crowds of

13. **A** players
B rivals
C spectators
D sportsmen

. The money raised is

14. **A** collected
B refused
C donated
D doled

to charity.

The rules are simple: two players take it in turns to

15. **A** swing
B slide
C flutter
D collide

their conker at their

opponent's nut. The winner is the player

16. **A** what
B which
C whom
D who

manages to smash their rival's conker. The

contest

17. **A** conducts
B operates
C happens
D manages

as a knockout, with the winning player from each game taking on the

winning player from another game, until only one player

18. **A** left
B lives
C stops
D remains

. Each year, the winners of

the men's and women's events are

19. **A** crowned
B honoured
C presented
D bestowed

King and Queen Conker. Entrants come from

all over the world, and previous winners have come from as far

20. **A** gone
B outside
C afield
D beyond

as Austria, Mexico

and Germany.

/ 12

Assessment Test 8

It was a chilly winter's day and Jo, Theo, Rosie, Alex and Ben were huddled around the blazing log fire in their living room. Ben and Jo were squabbling as usual — this time it was over what game to play. Ben wanted to play hide and seek, whereas Jo didn't want to stir from the cosy living room, and thought they should play a board game instead.

Theo sighed. Despite being two years younger than the twins, it always seemed to be his job to resolve their quarrels. As Ben's voice got louder and louder, Theo decided that it was time to step in.

"Look," he said, shouting to make himself heard, "I'll hide my pencil case somewhere in this room, then you can all hunt for it. Whoever finds it wins my turtle-shaped eraser."

Rosie, who was four years younger than Theo, had coveted the turtle eraser for weeks and she agreed immediately. Ben and Jo were both unwilling to concede defeat, but they finally gave in.

"Right, you all need to close your eyes while I hide it," ordered Theo. He glanced around his siblings to make sure none of them were looking. Alex still had his eyes open, but since he was only two Theo wasn't too concerned. Rosie was a year older than Alex and was more likely to peek, so Theo kept an eye on her as he cast his eyes around the room, searching for the perfect hiding place. Behind the curtains? Too obvious. Up the chimney? Not a chance! His eyes alighted on his youngest brother, playing with some glove puppets, and he knew he'd found the ideal spot.

Answer these questions about the text that you've just read.
Circle the letter that matches the correct answer.

21. Which of these statements cannot be true?

    A Ben was born before Theo.
    B Rosie is 6 years younger than Jo.
    C Theo is 8 years old.
    D Alex is 1 year younger than Rosie.

22. Why do you think Jo agrees to Theo's game?

    A She doesn't want to make him angry.
    B She is tired of arguing with Ben.
    C She wants to win Theo's eraser.
    D She wants to keep warm.

23. Why doesn't Theo hide his pencil case up the chimney?

    A Because he doesn't want to get it dirty.
    B Because he would get hurt.
    C Because he thinks it's too obvious.
    D Because the others will hear him doing it.

24. Why do you think Theo isn't worried that Alex has his eyes open?

    A He wants Alex to find the pencil case.
    B Alex isn't watching what he's doing.
    C He thinks Alex is too young to understand the game.
    D Alex is distracted by the glove puppets.

/ 4

Carry on to the next question → →

> Find the word that means the same, or nearly the same, as the word on the left.
>
> **Example:** **fantastic** <u>wonderful</u> awful acceptable expected

25. **split** close rift apart undo

26. **trick** sly lie fake ruse

27. **awful** extreme astonishing dire daunting

28. **risk** hazard dangerous inconvenience uncertain

29. **claw** grip paw talon injure

30. **adult** mature senior ripe grow

31. **leap** dive bound swing plunge

32. **wobble** indecisive bounce stray teeter

33. **take** stole seize carry choose

34. **shelter** secure hidden escape refuge

35. **pretend** feign assume mislead cheat

36. **silent** ignored mute vocal solemn

/ 12

> Complete the word on the right so that it means the opposite, or nearly the opposite, of the word on the left.
>
> **Example: dark** l i g h t

37. **enemy** ☐☐l y

38. **dear** ☐☐e☐p

39. **sociable** r☐☐☐☐v e d

40. **wise** i☐n☐r☐☐t

41. **lazy** i n☐☐s t r☐☐u s

42. **serious** ☐r i☐☐a l

43. **forever** ☐r☐☐f l y

44. **tall** s☐☐n☐☐d

/ 8

Assessment Test 8

Find the word that means the opposite, or nearly the opposite, of the word on the left.

Example: **big**   more   large   <u>little</u>   less

45. **sow**   knit   reap   dig   cut

46. **legal**   prison   immoral   criminal   dishonest

47. **land**   arrive   departing   cruise   ocean

48. **low**   elevated   steep   above   hover

49. **master**   assist   servant   child   helper

50. **past**   fail   late   destined   forthcoming

51. **real**   dead   indefinite   imitation   hidden

52. **clear**   vague   explicit   irregular   vacant

53. **few**   full   lacking   meagre   copious

54. **repel**   favour   disgust   entice   recall

55. **hide**   expose   overt   exhibition   report

56. **hopeful**   scared   eager   despair   pessimistic

/ 12

Total   / 56

End of Test

Assessment Test 8

Glossary

adjective	A word that <u>describes</u> a <u>noun</u>, e.g. '<u>beautiful</u> morning', '<u>frosty</u> lawn'.
adverb	A word that <u>describes</u> a <u>verb</u>, which often ends with the <u>suffix</u> '<u>-ly</u>', e.g. 'She laughed <u>happily</u>.', 'He ran <u>quickly</u>.'
antonym	A word that has the <u>opposite meaning</u> to another, e.g. the antonym of 'good' is 'bad'.
connective	A word that <u>joins</u> two clauses or sentences, e.g. '<u>and</u>', '<u>but</u>', '<u>therefore</u>'.
consonants	The <u>21 letters</u> of the alphabet that <u>aren't vowels</u>.
fiction	Text that has been <u>made up</u> by the author, about <u>imaginary people</u> and <u>events</u>.
homographs	Words that are spelt the same but have <u>different meanings</u>, e.g. 'I want to <u>play</u>.' and 'I saw a <u>play</u>.'
homophones	Words that <u>sound the same</u>, but mean different things, e.g. '<u>hair</u>' and '<u>hare</u>'.
imagery	Language that creates a <u>vivid picture</u> in the reader's mind.
metaphor	A way of <u>describing</u> something by saying that it <u>is</u> something else, e.g. 'John's legs were lead weights.'
multiple choice	A type of <u>11+ question</u> that gives you <u>answers</u> to choose from.
non-fiction	Text that is about <u>facts</u> and <u>real people</u> and <u>events</u>.
noun	A word that <u>names</u> something, e.g. '<u>Paul</u>', '<u>cat</u>', '<u>fear</u>', '<u>childhood</u>'.
personification	A way of describing something by giving it <u>human feelings</u> and <u>characteristics</u>, e.g. 'The cruel wind plucked remorselessly at my threadbare clothes.'
prefix	A string of letters that can be put <u>in front</u> of a word to <u>change its meaning</u>, e.g. '<u>un-</u>' can be added to '<u>lock</u>' to make '<u>unlock</u>'.
pronoun	Words that can be used <u>instead</u> of <u>nouns</u>, e.g. '<u>I</u>', '<u>you</u>', '<u>he</u>', '<u>it</u>'.
simile	A way of describing something by <u>comparing</u> it to something else, e.g. 'The stars were <u>like</u> a thousand diamonds, glittering in the sky.'
subject	The <u>person</u> or <u>thing doing</u> the action of a verb, e.g. '<u>Jo</u> laughed', '<u>the bird</u> flew'.
suffix	A string of letters that can be put <u>after</u> a word to <u>change its meaning</u>, e.g. '<u>-er</u>' can be added to the end of '<u>play</u>' to make '<u>player</u>'.
synonym	A word with a <u>similar meaning</u> to another word, e.g. '<u>big</u>' is a synonym of '<u>huge</u>'.
verb	An <u>action</u> or <u>doing</u> word, e.g. '<u>run</u>', '<u>went</u>', '<u>think</u>', or a <u>being</u> word, e.g. '<u>is</u>'.
vowels	The letters '<u>a</u>', '<u>e</u>', '<u>i</u>', '<u>o</u>' and '<u>u</u>'.

Answers

Page 2 — Plurals

1) **potatoes** — 'potato' becomes 'potatoes' — some words ending in 'o' add 'es' to make the plural.

2) **witnesses** — 'witness' becomes 'witnesses' — words ending in 'ss' often add 'es' to make the plural.

3) **leaves** — 'leaf' becomes 'leaves' — often words ending in 'f' lose the 'f' and add 'ves' to make the plural.

4) **foxes** — 'fox' becomes 'foxes' — often words ending in 'x' add 'es' to make the plural.

5) **canaries** — 'canary' becomes 'canaries' — when words end in 'y' and the letter before the 'y' is a consonant, 'y' is replaced with 'ies' to make the plural.

6) **sandwiches** — 'sandwich' becomes 'sandwiches' — often words ending in 'ch' add 'es' to make the plural.

7) **loaves** — 'loaf' becomes 'loaves' — often words ending in 'f' lose the 'f' and add 'ves' to make the plural.

8) **pizzas** — 'pizza' becomes 'pizzas' — most commonly, words add 's' to make the plural.

9) **teeth** — 'tooth' becomes 'teeth' — this is an irregular plural.

10) **men** — 'man' becomes 'men' — this is an irregular plural.

11) **people** — 'person' becomes 'people' — this is an irregular plural.

12) **geese** — 'goose' becomes 'geese' — this is an irregular plural.

13) **lice** — 'louse' becomes 'lice' — this is an irregular plural.

14) **feet** — 'foot' becomes 'feet' — this is an irregular plural.

15) **these** — 'this' becomes 'these' — this is an irregular plural.

16) **sheep** — 'sheep' does not change — this is an irregular plural.

Page 3 — Homophones

1) **our** — 'our' makes sense here — it means 'something belonging to us', whereas 'hour' is a unit of time.

2) **steel** — 'steel' makes sense here — it is a type of metal, whereas 'steal' means 'to take something without permission'.

3) **scent** — 'scent' makes sense here — it means 'fragrance', whereas 'sent' means 'made to go'.

4) **flour** — 'flour' makes sense here — it is ground wheat used for baking, whereas a 'flower' is 'a part of some plants'.

5) **pour** — 'pour' makes sense here — it refers to the act of tipping liquid from a container, whereas 'poor' means 'lacking wealth'.

6) **sail** — 'sail' makes sense here — it means 'to move on water using wind power', whereas 'sale' means 'the exchange of goods for money'.

7) **bare** — 'bare' makes sense here — it means 'uncovered', whereas 'bear' can mean a type of large animal or 'to tolerate'.

8) **fare** — 'fare' makes sense here — it means 'a payment for transport', whereas 'fair' means 'even-handed' or 'a show or carnival'.

9) **route** — 'route' makes sense here — it means 'the path of a journey', whereas a 'root' is the underground part of a plant.

10) **worn** — 'worn' makes sense here —it means 'damaged by overuse', whereas 'warn' means 'to make someone aware of a risk'.

11) **they're** — 'they're' makes sense here — it is a shortened version of 'they are'.

12) **their** — 'their' makes sense here — it means 'belonging to them'.

13) **there** — 'there' makes sense here — in this sentence it is used to refer to a particular place.

14) **there** — 'there' makes sense here — in this sentence it is used to refer to a particular place.

15) **their** — 'their' makes sense here — it means 'belonging to them'.

16) **they're** — 'they're' makes sense here — it is a shortened version of 'they are'.

Page 4 — Prefixes And Suffixes

1) **il** — The word is 'illogical'.

2) **im** — The word is 'immature'.

3) **il** — The word is 'illegal'.

4) **in** — The word is 'incapable'.

5) **im** — The word is 'imperfect'.

6) **in** — The word is 'inconsiderate'.

7) **im** — The word is 'implausible'.

8) **il** — The word is 'illegible'.

9) **retirement** — The suffix added is 'ment'.

10) **forgiveness** — The suffix added is 'ness'.

11) **useful** — The suffix added is 'ful'.

12) **treatment** — The suffix added is 'ment'.

13) **politeness** — The suffix added is 'ness'.

14) **agreement** — The suffix added is 'ment'.

15) **merriment** — The suffix added is 'ment', but you also need to replace the 'y' with an 'i'.

16) **beautiful** — The suffix added is 'ful', but you also need to replace the 'y' with an 'i'.

80

Page 5 — Awkward Spellings

1) **ie** — The word is 'thief'. The vowel sound rhymes with bee and it's not after 'c', so 'i' comes before 'e'.

2) **ie** — The word is 'priest'. The vowel sound rhymes with bee and it's not after 'c', so 'i' comes before 'e'.

3) **ei** — The word is 'receipt'. The vowel sound rhymes with bee and it's after 'c', so 'e' comes before 'i'.

4) **ie** — The word is 'fierce'. The vowel sound rhymes with bee and it's not after 'c', so 'i' comes before 'e'.

5) **ie** — The word is 'piece'. The vowel sound rhymes with bee and it's not after 'c', so 'i' comes before 'e'.

6) **ei** — The word is 'neither'. This is an exception to the 'i before e' rule. 'neither' doesn't always rhyme with 'bee' — it can be pronounced in different ways.

7) **ie** — The word is 'relieved'. The vowel sound rhymes with bee and it's not after 'c', so 'i' comes before 'e'.

8) **ie** — The word is 'pierced'. The vowel sound rhymes with bee and it's not after 'c', so 'i' comes before 'e'.

9) **s** — The word is 'history'.

10) **ll** — The word is 'allowed'.

11) **dd** — The word is 'address'.

12) **m** — The word is 'tomorrow'.

13) **cc** — The word is 'accepted'.

14) **c** — The word is 'necessary'.

15) **d** — The word is 'immediately'.

16) **cc** — The word is 'succeeded'.

Page 6 — Mixed Spelling Questions

1) **donkeys** — 'donkies' should be 'donkeys' — it ends in 'y' and there's a vowel before the 'y', so you just add 's' to make it plural.

2) **raspberries** — 'raspberrys' should be 'raspberries' — it ends in 'y' and there's a consonant before the 'y', so you change the 'y' to 'ies' to make it plural.

3) **knock** — 'nock' should be 'knock' — it has a silent 'k'.

4) **staircase** — 'starecase' should be 'staircase' — 'stair' means 'a set of steps', whereas 'stare' means 'to look intently'.

5) **guilty** — 'gilty' should be 'guilty' — many words containing a 'g' have a 'u' between the 'g' and the next vowel — 'guess' is another example.

6) **sandwich** — 'sanwich' should be 'sandwich' — there's a 'd' after the 'n'.

7) **recommend** — 'reccommend' should be 'recommend' — it has one 'c' and two 'm's.

8) **their** — 'there' should be 'their' — it means 'belonging to them'.

9) **weigh** — 'wiegh' should be 'weigh' — the vowel sound doesn't rhyme with 'bee', so 'e' comes before 'i'.

10) **sun** — 'son' should be 'sun' — the sentence refers to the star in our solar system, not a male child.

11) **wonderful** — 'wonderfull' should be 'wonderful' — it has a single 'l' at the end.

12) **competition** — 'compitition' should be 'competition' — the root word is 'compete'.

13) **protein** — 'protien' should be 'protein' — it is an exception to the rule: 'i before e except after c, but only when it rhymes with b'.

14) **actually** — 'actualy' should be 'actually' — it should have a double 'l' in the middle.

15) **inefficient** — 'imefficient' should be 'inefficient' — the prefix is 'in'.

16) **collection** — 'collectian' should be 'collection' — the suffix is 'ion'.

17) **excitement** — 'excitment' should be 'excitement' — the root word is 'excite' and it keeps the final 'e' when the suffix 'ment' is added.

18) **secretary** — 'secratary' should be 'secretary' — it has an 'e' in the middle.

Page 7 — Mixed Spelling Questions

1) **to** — 'to' makes sense here because it is a preposition linking the nouns 'Kate' and 'people'.

2) **too** — 'too' makes sense here because it refers to something excessive.

3) **whether** — 'whether' makes sense here because it expresses a choice between alternatives.

4) **weather** — 'weather' makes sense here because it means 'atmospheric conditions', e.g. what the temperature is and whether it's raining.

5) **borrow** — 'borrow' makes sense here because it means 'to receive something as a temporary loan'.

6) **lend** — 'lend' makes sense here because it means 'to give something as a temporary loan'.

7) **wear** — 'wear' makes sense here because it is a verb meaning 'to have on the body'.

8) **where** — 'where' makes sense here because it is an adverb which shows location.

9) **worse** — 'worse' makes sense here because it is a comparative adjective.

10) **worst** — 'worst' makes sense here because it is a superlative adjective.

11) **well** — 'well' makes sense here because it is an adverb describing the verb 'done'.

12) **good** — 'good' makes sense here because it is an adjective describing Chunni's ability to make friends.

13) **lose** — 'lose' makes sense here because it means 'to fail'.

14) **loose** — 'loose' makes sense here because it means 'not tight'.

15) **dessert** — 'dessert' makes sense here — it has a double 's' in the middle when it refers to a pudding.

16) **desert** — 'desert' makes sense here — it has a single 's' in the middle when it refers to a dry and barren land.

17) **who** — 'who' makes sense here because it refers to a person.

18) **which** — 'which' makes sense here because it refers to an object.

Answers

Page 8 — Verbs

1) **went** — The sentence should be 'Cerys **went** to the doctor's last night.' This is the correct past tense form of the verb 'to go'.

2) **made** — The sentence should be 'Blacksmiths have **made** horseshoes for centuries.' This is the correct option to complete the verb phrase 'have made'.

3) **having** — The sentence should be 'Divyesh is **having** a bouncy-castle party on Sunday afternoon.' This is the correct option to complete the verb phrase 'is having'.

4) **was** — The sentence should be 'I **was** just finishing my homework when the doorbell rang.' This correctly completes the verb phrase 'was finishing' and it agrees with the noun 'I'.

5) **broken** — The sentence should be '"It has **broken**!" cried Mahmud mournfully.' This is the correct option to complete the verb phrase 'has broken'.

6) **talked** — The sentence should be 'The sailor **talked** until the sun rose about his time at sea.' This is the correct past tense form of the verb 'to talk'.

7) **fallen** — The sentence should be 'Grace had **fallen** over and landed in the mud.' This is the correct option to complete the verb phrase 'had fallen'.

8) **feel** — The sentence should be 'Corned beef makes me **feel** ill.' This is the correct option to complete the verb phrase 'makes me feel'.

9) **drove** — The sentence should be 'He **drove** to school in a go-kart yesterday.' This is the correct past tense form of the verb 'to drive".

10) **laughs** — The sentence should be 'My nephew always **laughs** when I tickle him.' This is the correct present tense form of the verb 'to laugh' and it agrees with the noun 'nephew'.

11) **saw** — The sentence should be 'I **saw** where the group of runners went.' This is the correct past tense form of the verb 'to see'.

12) **was** — The sentence should be 'It **was** forbidden to enter the courtyard when the gate was shut.' This is the correct past tense form of the verb 'to be' and it agrees with the pronoun 'It'.

13) **heard** — The sentence should be 'He **heard** the steam train before he could see it.' This is the correct past tense form of the verb 'to hear'.

14) **is** — The sentence should be 'Salami **is** a type of cured meat eaten with bread.' This is the correct present tense form of the verb 'to be' and it agrees with the noun 'Salami'.

15) **spin** — The sentence should be 'Lottie watched the spider **spin** its web.' This is the correct form of the verb 'to spin'.

16) **sung** — The sentence should be 'The choir had **sung** the piece many times before.' This is the correct option to complete the verb phrase 'had sung'.

17) **began** — The sentence should be 'Once Ben **began** writing the story, he couldn't stop.' This is the correct past tense form of the verb 'to begin'.

18) **bought** — The sentence should be 'I **bought** these apples at the market.' This is the correct past tense form of the verb 'to buy'.

Page 9 — Verbs And Connectives

1) **don't** (or **do not**) — The sentence should be 'Matt still gets annoyed when people **don't** tidy up.' This is the correct present tense form of the verb 'to do' and it agrees with the noun 'people'.

2) **flew** (or **was flying**) — The sentence should be 'Beth felt quite travel sick when she **flew** to Australia.' This is the correct past tense form of the verb 'to fly' and it agrees with the noun 'Beth'.

3) **went** (or **was going**) — The sentence should be 'I **went** to the theme park with my cousins yesterday.' This is the correct past tense form of the verb 'to go'.

4) **knocked** — The sentence should be 'He was annoyed when the dog **knocked** over his drink.' This is the correct past tense form of the verb 'to knock'.

5) **speak** — The sentence should be 'My dad can **speak** six languages, including Mandarin.' This is the correct option to complete the verb phrase 'can speak'.

6) **passed** — The sentence should be 'My goldfish was delighted when she **passed** her driving test.' This is the correct past tense form of the verb 'to pass'.

7) **left** — The sentence should be 'I **left** my P.E. kit in the changing rooms last week.' This is the correct past tense form of the verb 'to leave'.

8) **said** — The sentence should be '"Take that back!" **said** Amara as she slammed the door.' This is the correct past tense form of the verb 'to say'.

9) **because** — The sentence should be 'I don't want to come to the park, **because** it is snowing.'

10) **so** — The sentence should be 'Hand me the hammer **so** I can hang this picture.'

11) **and** — The sentence should be 'Over the weekend, I went swimming **and** I went ice skating.'

12) **before** — The sentence should be 'Put your coat on **before** you leave the house.'

13) **or** — The sentence should be 'We can have our pudding now **or** we can wait until later.'

14) **until** — The sentence should be 'Don't open your present **until** your mum arrives.'

15) **whereas** — The sentence should be 'Maisie went to school **whereas** her brother stayed at home.'

16) **unless** — The sentence should be 'You can't come in **unless** you've brought cake.'

82

Page 10 — Mixed Grammar Questions

1) **quickly** — The sentence should be 'Aisha enjoyed cycling **quickly** around the duck pond.'

2) **eat** — The sentence should be 'We decided to **eat** our picnic under the large beech tree.'

3) **was** — The sentence should be 'I saw the ginger kitten when he **was** prowling in the garden.'

4) **We** — The sentence should be '**We** travelled to Hawaii with our pet mouse.'

5) **swim** — The sentence should be 'Are you going to **swim** across the English Channel?'

6) **any** — The sentence should be 'I don't want **any** chips with my burger.'

7) **was** — The sentence should be 'When I **was** five, I fell out of a bedroom window.'

8) **my** — The sentence should be 'Melinda (the woman with blonde hair) is **my** sister-in-law.'

9) **noun** — 'nurse' is a noun because it is the name of a profession.

10) **verb** — 'danced' is a verb because it is an action word in the sentence.

11) **verb** — 'Listen' is a verb because it is an action word in the sentence.

12) **adjective** — 'impressive' is an adjective — it describes the noun the 'chess player'.

13) **adverb** — 'Suddenly' is an adverb — it describes the verb 'capsized'.

14) **noun** — 'clue' is a noun — it is the name for something.

15) **connective** — 'while' is a connective — it connects two clauses.

16) **adverb** — 'quickly' is an adverb — it describes how he pulled the rope.

Page 11 — Multiple Meanings

1) **sweet** — 'sweet' can mean 'flavoured with sugar' or 'good-natured'.

2) **play** — 'play' can mean 'a theatrical performance' or 'to be merry or lively'.

3) **tight** — 'tight' can mean 'not much room' or 'reluctant to spend money'.

4) **top** — 'top' can mean 'the highest point' or 'a cover for a jar or can'.

5) **upset** — 'upset' can mean 'to tip over' or 'to make unhappy'.

6) **cold** — 'cold' can mean 'lacking heat' or 'unaffectionate'.

7) **simple** — 'simple' can mean 'not elaborate' or 'not difficult'.

8) **present** — 'present' can mean 'at this time' or 'something given as a gesture of goodwill'.

9) **form** — 'form' can mean 'a group in a school' or 'a set of questions'.

10) **kind** — 'kind' can mean 'gentle or pleasant' or 'a type of something'.

11) **match** — 'match' can mean 'a sporting competition' or 'an alliance of two people'.

12) **sign** — 'sign' can mean 'to write your name' or 'an information notice'.

13) **second** — 'second' can mean 'a short amount of time' or 'following the leader'.

14) **key** — 'key' can mean 'something that is essential' or 'an explanation of symbols or codes'.

15) **band** — 'band' can mean 'a group which plays instruments' or 'a ring-shaped object'.

16) **refuse** — 'refuse' can mean 'trash' or 'to say no to something'.

17) **row** — 'row' can mean 'to argue' or 'to propel a boat'.

18) **sow** — 'sow' can mean 'a female pig' or 'to put in the ground for growing'.

Page 12 — Closest Meaning

1) **cross** — Both words mean 'annoyed'.

2) **nice** — Both words mean 'pleasant'.

3) **purchase** — Both words mean 'to acquire using money'.

4) **hideous** — Both words mean 'unattractive'.

5) **permit** — Both words mean 'to give permission'.

6) **murmur** — Both words mean 'to speak quietly'.

7) **amusing** — Both words mean 'comical'.

8) **garbage** — Both words mean 'rubbish or refuse'.

9) **valuable** — Both words mean 'of high value'.

10) **truthful** — Both words mean 'sincere'.

11) **downpour** — Both words are types of wet weather.

12) **identical** — Both words mean 'alike'.

13) **hope** — Both words mean 'to desire'.

14) **chart** — Both are ways of presenting data visually.

15) **sly** — Both words mean 'crafty'.

16) **amiable** — Both words mean 'warm and likeable'.

17) **neat** — Both words mean 'ordered'.

18) **pardon** — Both words mean 'to excuse someone's wrongdoing'.

Answers

Page 13 — Closest Meaning

1) **va**s**t** — Both words mean 'of considerable size'.

2) **boi**lin**g** — Both words mean 'a high temperature'.

3) we**ep** — Both words mean 'to sob'.

4) fi**nish** — Both words mean 'to end something'.

5) pl**unge** — Both words mean 'to drop to a lower level without control'.

6) **fa**ls**e** — Both words mean 'not real'.

7) **chi**ll**y** — Both words mean 'a low temperature'.

8) **chub**by — Both words mean 'overweight'.

9) su**perb** — Both words mean 'great'.

10) **a**dore — Both words mean 'to cherish'.

11) in**fo**rm — Both words mean 'to pass on information'.

12) str**ang**e — Both words mean 'odd'.

13) quer**y** — Both words mean 'to ask for an answer'.

14) **d**rea**dful** — Both words mean 'not good'.

15) c**oars**e — Both words mean 'not smooth'.

16) f**u**rious — Both words mean 'cross'.

17) b**rie**f — Both words mean 'not long'.

18) **d**a**ring** — Both words mean 'courageous'.

Page 14 — Opposite Meaning

1) **downstairs** — 'upstairs' means 'on a higher floor', whereas 'downstairs' means 'on a lower floor'.

2) **filthy** — 'clean' means 'not dirty', whereas 'filthy' means 'dirty'.

3) **old** — 'young' means 'youthful', whereas 'old' means 'elderly'.

4) **repulsive** — 'beautiful' means 'attractive', whereas 'repulsive' means 'very unattractive'.

5) **empty** — 'full' means 'at capacity', whereas 'empty' means 'having no content'.

6) **narrow** — 'wide' means 'broad', whereas 'narrow' means 'thin'.

7) **loathe** — 'love' means 'adore', whereas 'loathe' means 'hate'.

8) **shallow** — 'deep' means 'extending a long way down', whereas 'shallow' means 'lacking depth'.

9) **dull** — 'shiny' means 'bright and gleaming', whereas 'dull' means 'matt or lacking colour'.

10) **squash** — 'stretch' means 'to pull apart', whereas 'squash' means 'to push together'.

11) **wealthy** — 'poor' means 'lacking money', whereas 'wealthy' means 'having lots of money'.

12) **buy** — 'sell' means 'to give goods in exchange for money', whereas 'buy' means 'to give money in exchange for goods'.

13) **major** — 'minor' means 'less important', whereas 'major' means 'more important'.

14) **costly** — 'cheap' means 'inexpensive', whereas 'costly' means 'expensive'.

15) **friend** — 'enemy' means 'someone who is disliked', whereas 'friend' means 'someone who is known and liked'.

16) **quiet** — 'busy' means 'crowded', whereas 'quiet' means 'free from crowds'.

17) **slack** — 'taut' means 'tight', whereas 'slack' means 'loose'.

18) **flat** — 'bumpy' means 'uneven', whereas 'flat' means 'even'.

Page 15 — Opposite Meaning

1) **par**t**ia**l — 'whole' means 'complete', whereas 'partial' means 'incomplete'.

2) de**cea**se**d** — 'alive' means 'living', whereas 'deceased' means 'not living'.

3) **qui**c**k** — 'slow' means 'at low speed', whereas 'quick' means 'at high speed'.

4) **whis**p**er** — 'shout' means 'to speak loudly', whereas 'whisper' means 'to speak quietly'.

5) **bold** — 'shy' means 'not confident', whereas 'bold' means 'confident'.

6) **dona**te — 'take' means 'to seize', whereas 'donate' means 'to give to someone else'.

7) **n**oi**s**y — 'quiet' means 'without noise', whereas 'noisy' means 'with lots of noise'.

8) **solu**t**io**n — 'problem' means 'difficulty', whereas 'solution' means 'to overcome a difficulty'.

9) stan**dar**d — 'different' means 'varied', whereas 'standard' means 'not varied'.

10) **c**o**mm**on — 'rare' means 'scarce', whereas 'common' means 'widespread'.

11) res**pon**d — 'question' means 'to ask', whereas 'respond' means 'to reply'.

12) **fu**ture — 'past' means 'before the present time', whereas 'future' means 'after the present time'.

13) cl**ou**dy — 'clear' means 'free from clouds', whereas 'cloudy' means 'obscured by clouds'.

14) p**o**l**ite** — 'rude' means 'discourteous', whereas 'polite' means 'courteous'.

15) e**xtend** — 'shorten' means 'to reduce in size', whereas 'extend' means 'to increase in size'.

16) **dist**ant — 'close' means 'nearby', whereas 'distant' means 'faraway'.

17) c**urve**d — 'straight' means 'without a bend', whereas 'curved' means 'bent'.

18) c**reate** — 'destroy' means 'to demolish', whereas 'create' means 'to build'.

Page 16 — Odd One Out

1) **numbers** — The other three are examples of numbers.

2) **warm** — The other three mean 'lacking heat'.

3) **hate** — The other three mean 'to feel positively about something'.

4) **mutter** — The other three all mean 'to speak loudly'.

5) **office** — The other three are all places where people live.

6) **glacier** — The other three are places where trees grow.

7) **oak** — The other three are types of flowers.

8) **fridge** — The other three are appliances used to heat food.

9) **slide** — The other three are all types of sport.

10) **recorder** — The other three are all stringed instruments.

11) **shorts** — The other three are all items of clothing worn to keep warm.

12) **chuckle** — The other three all mean 'joyful'.

13) **gloves** — The other three are all things you wear on your feet.

14) **diced** — The other three are all ways of cooking.

15) **song** — The other three are all types of pictures.

16) **plastic** — The other three are all natural materials.

17) **rehearsal** — The other three are all types of performance.

18) **come** — The other three all mean 'to depart'.

Page 17 — Reorder Words To Make A Sentence

Your child may have made a different sentence using the words given. This is fine, as long as the correct word has been chosen.

1) **snow** — The words can be rearranged into the sentence 'My favourite season is winter.'

2) **stables** — The words can be rearranged into the sentence 'I rode to school on a donkey.'

3) **pages** — The words can be rearranged into the sentence 'Read this book for your homework.'

4) **traffic** — The words can be rearranged into the sentence 'Look both ways when you cross the road.'

5) **study** — The words can be rearranged into the sentence 'Maths and Science are my favourite subjects.'

6) **run** — The words can be rearranged into the sentence 'The cat darted under the wooden table.'

7) **tent** — The words can be rearranged into the sentence 'Last summer we went camping in France.'

8) **laces** — The words can be rearranged into the sentence 'Put your socks on before your shoes.'

9) **foreign** — The words can be rearranged into the sentence 'I want to learn to speak Italian.'

10) **crunch** — The words can be rearranged into the sentence 'The ogre munched on a red apple.'

11) **watch** — The words can be rearranged into the sentence 'The circus opens tomorrow night.'

12) **pitch** — The words can be rearranged into the sentence 'The referee blew his whistle at the end'.

13) **station** — The words can be rearranged into the sentence 'We will not make it there on time.'

14) **has** — The words can be rearranged into the sentence 'We have a pet mongoose called Eric.'

15) **ran** — The words can be rearranged into the sentence 'The barge sailed gracefully down the canal.'

16) **morning** — The words can be rearranged into the sentence 'Gemma got up early to go wrestling.'

17) **journey** — The words can be rearranged into the sentence 'I am taking the bus to school tomorrow.'

18) **office** — The words can be rearranged into the sentence 'The postman carried his bag of letters.'

Page 18 — Using Rules Of English

1) **until** — The sentence should be 'I am going to watch TV until Nassrin arrives.'

2) **borrow** — The sentence should be 'When I forgot my pen, Zane said I could borrow one of his.'

3) **slowly** — The sentence should be 'He slowly raised his hand to answer the question.'

4) **love** — The sentence should be 'Luke used to love eating pancakes for breakfast.'

5) **thoughtful** — The sentence should be 'I was grateful for his thoughtful present.'

6) **what** — The sentence should be 'I always wondered what lay beyond the mansion's gates.'

7) **found** — The sentence should be 'I found the day at the museum interesting.'

8) **stuck** — The sentence should be 'When we made paper lanterns, the glue stuck to my fingers.'

9) **through** — The sentence should be 'We had to pass through a security scanner to reach the departure lounge.'

10) **best** — The sentence should be 'Of all my friends, I know you the best.'

11) **her** — The sentence should be 'Tamara won the medal; it was her third victory this year.'

12) **into** — The sentence should be 'I cracked the egg into the cake batter.'

13) **serious** — The sentence should be 'My teacher looked serious when he told me to stop talking.'

14) **our** — The sentence should be 'When my family go on holiday, we take our own towels.'

15) Although — The sentence should be 'Although I had a fever, I came first in the egg-and-spoon race.'

16) theirs — The sentence should be 'Marc threw the ball, and then the whistle blew; the trophy was theirs.'

17) brought — The sentence should be 'Manjit brought crisps and sandwiches to the garden party'.

18) longer — The sentence should be 'This week's play was longer than last week's.'

Page 19 — Choose A Word

1) nervously — 'Marco waited **nervously** at the side of the pool.'

2) lining — 'Five other swimmers were **lining** up'

3) took — 'He snapped his goggles on and **took** a deep breath.'

4) if — 'He had to win this race **if** his school was to stand any chance of winning the competition.'

5) currently — 'The tallest building in the world is **currently** the Burj Khalifa'

6) Completed — '**Completed** in 2009'

7) measures — 'it **measures** over 828 m'

8) height — 'twice the **height** of the Empire State Building.'

9) first — 'Martial arts were **first** practised over 4,000 years ago'

10) reasons —'Today, there are many **reasons**'

11) fit — 'Some people practise martial arts to stay **fit**'

12) balance — 'others find that it helps their coordination and **balance**'.

Page 20 — Choose A Word

1) seriously — 'Ancient Romans took their food very **seriously**'

2) lavish — 'wealthy citizens would hold **lavish** feasts for their guests.'

3) If — '**If** you were a guest at a Roman feast'

4) served — 'you might have been **served** dormouse'

5) popular — 'many ingredients used in Roman cooking are still **popular** today.'

6) at — 'Jennifer opened her curtains and gazed **at** the glistening white carpet'

7) window — 'covered the ground below her **window**'

8) hidden — 'The garden path was **hidden** under a frosty blanket'

9) dangled — 'sparkling icicles **dangled** from the shed roof.'

10) glee — 'Her heart leapt with **glee**'

Page 21 — Fill In Missing Letters

1) raised — 'Pupils and teachers at Mossbridge School have **raised** over £500'.

2) successful — 'after a **successful** summer fair.'

3) field — 'The fair was held on the school playing **field**'.

4) visitors — 'attracting over 200 **visitors**.'

5) prizes — 'a raffle with a variety of great **prizes**.'

6) brilliant — 'It was a **brilliant** day'.

7) country — 'In this **country**'

8) Other — '**Other** countries and cultures have their own lucky symbols.'

9) fortune — 'the number 8 is meant to bring good **fortune**'

10) capital — 'held in China's **capital** city, Beijing'

11) prevent — 'they would **prevent** a home'

12) struck — 'from being **struck** by lightning.'

13) clock — 'The **clock** struck six'

14) slippers — 'Beth put a pair of **slippers** down to warm.'

15) everyone — '**everyone** brightened to welcome her.'

16) stopped — 'Meg **stopped** lecturing'

17) forgot — 'Jo **forgot** how tired she was'

18) nearer — 'she sat up to hold the slippers **nearer** to the blaze.'

Page 22 — Fill In Missing Letters

1) buildings — 'Like most of the **buildings** in London'

2) timber — 'the bakery was made from **timber**'

3) neighbouring — 'engulfed the **neighbouring** structures'

4) uncontrollable — 'the fire became **uncontrollable**.'

5) through — 'the fire raged **through** the city'

6) tragedy — 'This **tragedy** became known as the Great Fire of London'.

7) catch — 'the professor would **catch** a train to work in the morning'

8) evening — 'in the **evening** Hachiko would go to the station'

9) **mas**ter — 'wait for his **master** to return.'

10) **jou**rney — 'he never made the return **journey**'

11) **wai**ted — 'Hachiko **waited** at the station for the professor.'

12) loy**alt**y — 'Hachiko is still remembered in Japan for his **loyalty**.'

13) fou**nd** — 'Alice opened the door and **found** that it led into a small passage'

14) **kn**elt — 'she **knelt** down and looked along the passage'

15) **long**ed — 'How she **longed** to get out of that dark hall'

16) wan**der** — '**wander** about among those beds of bright flowers'

17) d**oor**way — 'she could not even get her head through the **doorway**'

18) sh**oul**ders — 'it would be of very little use without my **shoulders**.'

Page 23 — Finding Hidden Facts

1) **Lisa** — Lisa goes riding three times a week: on Saturday, Sunday and Wednesday.

2) **William** — William is only going on one holiday: cycling with Mark.

3) **Haj** — Haj likes three toppings: raisins, lemon curd and sausages.

4) **Edward** — Edward only has two activities planned: swimming and shopping.

Pages 24 & 25 — Multiple-Statement Questions — Logic

1) **D** — Max runs faster than Charlotte, and Ahmed is slower than Charlotte, so Max must run faster than Ahmed.

2) **B** — Josh's house has half as many bedrooms as Karl's house, so Karl's house can't have 5 bedrooms because Josh's can't have 2.5 rooms.

3) **D** — Jamie was born before Georgia, Laura and Rohan, so he's the oldest.

4) **D** — July was 7 degrees hotter than June, and August was only 2 degrees hotter than June, so July can't have been cooler than August.

5) **B** — Patrick's bus arrived at 7.15, Hannah's bus arrived 10 minutes later at 7.25, and Jacob's bus arrived 15 minutes after Hannah's, so Jacob's bus arrived at 7.40.

6) **C** — Lucy buys four banners for £3 each, so she spends a total of £12. Lily spends half as much as Lucy, so she spends £6. Grace and Dan spend £20 between them, and Dan spends £6.50, so Grace must spend £13.50, which is £7.50 more than Lily.

Page 26 — Understanding The Language In The Text

1) **C** — The duvet is described as a cave to show that it is in the same shape as a cave.

2) **C** — "hissed" means 'to talk quietly' — Haji is trying not to disturb whatever he thinks he has seen beneath his desk.

3) **A** — Describing Haji's heartbeat as a drum thumping suggests it was loud because a drumbeat is often loud.

4) **A** — The image of the curtains "whispering" suggests they're moving gently.

5) **B** — The word "growl" suggests that the creature is threatening.

Pages 27-29 — Mixed Comprehension Questions

1) **D** — In the passage it says that "many parts have fallen into disrepair".

2) **C** — In the passage it says that the wall "marked the northernmost boundary of the Roman Empire".

3) **B** — In the passage it says that forts had "temples, granaries, bath houses and even hospitals", but it doesn't mention tax offices.

4) **C** — In the passage it says there were "occasional attacks from the north".

5) **D** — In the passage it says that "Antoninus believed that it would help the Romans conquer Scotland".

6) **D** — In the passage it says that the wall might have been used "to control immigration", not to increase it.

7) **A** — In the passage it says Hadrian's Wall is "the longest wall in Europe", not the longest in the world.

8) **C** — 'power' is closest in meaning to "might". Both words mean 'strength'.

9) **A** — 'withdrew' is closest in meaning to "retreated". Both words mean 'moved back'.

10) **D** — "his efforts were fruitless" means that he didn't achieve what he wanted to, so he was 'unsuccessful'.

Pages 30-35 — Assessment Test 1

1) **D** — In the passage it says that Gary Dahl was "an advertising executive", which means that he worked in advertising.

2) **B** — In the passage it says that "after 1975, sales dried up".

3) **C** — In the passage it says that Pet Rocks don't need "feeding, walking or bathing", and won't incur "any expensive vet bills".

4) **D** — The instruction booklet didn't tell you how to make a bed of straw.

5) **A** — In the passage it says "Pet Rocks sold well during the Christmas period", and "after 1975, sales dried up", so they sold well in December 1975.

6) **C** — In the passage it says "they were destined to be a fad". This means that people lost interest in them.

7) **D** — He came up with an idea that people wouldn't expect to do well but he made a lot of money from it.

8) **C** — 'original' is closest in meaning to "unique". Both words mean 'not based on anything else'.

9) **B** — 'short-lived trend' is closest in meaning to "fad". Both words mean 'a craze that doesn't last'.

10) **A** — "sales dried up" means that people stopped buying Pet Rocks.

11) **D** — Pet Rocks sold well at Christmas because they were a popular novelty gift.

12) **C** — This phrase means 'to be well-known around the globe'.

13) **sunset** — 'sunrise' means 'dawn', whereas 'sunset' means 'dusk'.

14) **light** — 'heavy' means 'weighing a lot', whereas 'light' means 'weighing little'.

15) **girl** — 'boy' means 'a young male', whereas 'girl' means 'a young female'.

16) **conclusion** — 'introduction' means 'beginning', whereas 'conclusion' means 'end'.

17) **winter** — 'summer' is the hottest season, whereas 'winter' is the coldest season.

18) **always** — 'never' means 'not ever', whereas 'always' means 'all the time'.

19) **demolish** — 'build' means 'to construct', whereas 'demolish' means 'to tear down'.

20) **risky** — 'safe' means 'not dangerous', whereas 'risky' means 'dangerous'.

21) **sharp** — Both words mean 'spiky'.

22) **hasty** — Both words mean 'speedy'.

23) **slender** — Both words mean 'thin'.

24) **sleepy** — Both words mean 'drowsy'.

25) **delayed** — Both words mean 'not on time'.

26) **centre** — Both words mean 'the half-way point'.

27) **brainy** — Both words mean 'intelligent'.

28) **injure** — Both words mean 'to harm'.

29) **school** — 'Ashok and Ben left **school**'

30) **stayed** — 'They had **stayed** late for hockey practice'

31) **changed** — 'Ben had taken ages to get **changed**'

32) **uncle** — 'Ashok's aunt and **uncle** were coming round for dinner'

33) **home** — 'he had to get **home** quickly.'

34) **field** — 'The boys jogged across the playing **field**'

35) **compete** — 'the tournament they were due to **compete** in on Saturday.'

36) **suddenly** — '"Come on," said Ben **suddenly**'

37) **time** — 'We'll be home in no **time**.'

38) **corner** — 'As the boys rounded the **corner**'

39) **strange** — 'they noticed a **strange** glow'

40) **large** — 'the **large** industrial bins'

41) **open** — 'The lid of the bin was propped **open**.'

42) **looked** — 'they saw what **looked** like a huge egg'

43) **wrapped** — 'half **wrapped** in an old sack'

44) **coming** — 'The eerie glow was **coming** from the egg'

45) **mini** — The other three all mean 'above average size'.

46) **badger** — The other three are all pets.

47) **finger** — The other three are all facial features.

48) **scarf** — The other three are all items of jewellery.

49) **apple** — The other three are all vegetables.

50) **work** — The other three involve using your voice.

51) **solo** — Both of these mean 'by yourself'.

52) **damp** — Both of these mean 'moist'.

53) **minuscule** — Both of these mean 'tiny'.

54) **joyous** — Both of these mean 'joyful'.

55) **sprint** — Both of these mean 'to move fast on foot'.

56) **sketch** — Both of these mean 'to depict something, usually in pencil'.

Pages 36-41 — Assessment Test 2

1) **D** — They were confused by this particular clue — it is a "mystery".

2) **C** — Jimmy felt as if he had read the clue a hundred times, because he had read it repeatedly and his team were finding it difficult to solve.

3) **B** — In this context "weakly" means 'half-heartedly'. He wants Felicity to remain positive about solving the clue but he doesn't have much hope.

4) **C** — In the passage it says "Park Hill School's annual camping trip". The word "annual" means 'once a year'.

5) **A** — In the passage it says "listening to ghost stories around the campfire", but 'building campfires' isn't mentioned specifically.

6) **C** — In the passage it says that Freddie was "infamous for being a bad loser".

7) **B** — Jimmy's team feel hopeful because they might have solved the last clue.

8) **A** — 'annoyance' is closest in meaning to "frustration". Both words mean 'a feeling of being fed up'.

9) **C** — 'dishonest' is closest in meaning to "underhand". Both words mean 'deceptive or unfair'.

10) **D** — 'uncertainly' is closest in meaning to "tentatively". Both words mean 'hesitantly'.

11) **C** — When Felicity suggests Westbury Farm, the group makes the connection between the clues 'coop' and 'fowl' and the farm. This is suggested by the final sentence of the passage.

12) **B** — 'Blue' means 'sad' or 'depressed' so this phrase means 'you won't be unhappy'.

13) **shore** — Both of these mean the area where the land meets the sea.

14) **jewel** — Both of these are words for precious minerals.

15) **jacket** — Both of these are outer garments with sleeves, worn on the top half of the body.

16) **smirk** — Both of these are facial expressions which show happiness.

17) **tempest** — Both words describe strong winds and rain.

18) **imitate** — Both words mean 'to do the same thing'.

19) **prank** — Both words mean 'a hoax'.

20) **prepared** — Both words mean 'able to start immediately'.

21) **feeble** — Both words mean 'not strong'.

22) **reduce** — Both words mean 'to lessen in size'.

23) **near** — 'far' means 'at a great distance', whereas 'near' means 'close by'.

24) **cease** — 'start' means 'to begin', whereas 'cease' means 'to stop'.

25) **giggle** — 'to weep' shows sadness, whereas 'to giggle' shows happiness.

26) **gangling** — 'short' means 'below average height', whereas 'gangling' means 'above average height'.

27) **listen** — 'speak' means 'to talk', whereas 'listen' means 'to try to hear'.

28) **vanish** — 'appear' means 'to emerge', whereas 'vanish' means 'to disappear'.

29) **diseased** — 'healthy' means 'well', whereas 'diseased' means 'unwell'.

30) **stale** — 'fresh' means 'new', whereas 'stale' means 'old'.

31) **grief** — 'joy' means 'happiness', whereas 'grief' means 'sadness'.

32) **stand** — 'lie' means 'to be horizontal', whereas 'stand' means 'to be vertical'.

33) **A** — 'Trudy had thought it would be **easy** to make a campfire.'

34) **C** — 'Earlier, she had **collected** a pile of sticks'

35) **C** — 'she had arranged **into** a wigwam shape.'

36) **A** — 'because **they** refused to catch fire.'

37) **B** — 'Trudy struck her **last** match'

38) **B** — 'held it gently **against** the smallest twigs.'

39) **C** — 'For a moment **nothing** happened.'

40) **A** — 'Trudy saw a plume of smoke **rising** from one corner.'

41) **C** — 'Quickly, she added **more** twigs to the pile.'

42) **A** — 'the pile of sticks **became** a cheerful, crackling blaze'

43) **B** — 'became a cheerful, **crackling** blaze.'

44) **A** — 'held her chilly hands out towards the warm glow **of** her fire.'

45) **egg** — The words can be rearranged into the sentence 'All the chickens have escaped.'

46) **camping** — The words can be rearranged into the sentence 'Climbing mountains is very hard work.'

47) **birthday** — The words can be rearranged into the sentence 'We went to that restaurant last year.'

48) **win** — The words can be rearranged into the sentence 'Kell is competing in the marathon today'.

49) **so** — The words can be rearranged into the sentence 'I was too tired to clean my bedroom.'

50) **rug** — The words can be rearranged into the sentence 'Sasha built a fort out of pillows.'

51) **together** — 'apart' means 'separate', whereas 'together' means 'in the same place'.

52) **base** — 'top' means 'the highest point', whereas 'base' means 'the lowest point'.

53) **daughter** — 'son' means 'a male child', whereas 'daughter' means 'a female child'.

54) **early** — 'late' means 'after an agreed time', whereas 'early' means 'before an agreed time'.

55) **cruel** — 'kind' means 'gentle', whereas 'cruel' means 'brutal'.

56) **valley** — 'hill' means 'the high point of a landscape', whereas 'valley' means 'the low point of a landscape'.

Pages 42-47 — Assessment Test 3

1) **A** — The spider tries to tempt the fly by telling her how lovely his parlour is.

2) **B** — In the poem the spider says he has "many curious things" in his parlour. "curious things" means 'interesting objects'.

3) **D** — In the poem the fly says "who goes up your winding stair can ne'er come down again."

4) **D** — In the poem the spider says "you must be weary, dear, with soaring up so high". "weary" means the same as 'tired'.

5) **B** — The fly doesn't trust the spider because she thinks he's trying to trap her.

6) **A** — In the poem, the spider tells the fly "you shall behold yourself" in the looking glass on the parlour shelf.

7) **C** — The spider is very complimentary to the fly in the third verse.

8) **C** — 'thin and transparent' is closest in meaning to "gauzy".

9) **B** — 'view' is closest in meaning to "behold". Both words mean 'to observe'.

10) **B** — 'amusing' could replace "witty". Both words mean 'funny'.

11) **C** — The spider is disappointed because he wants the fly to come into his parlour, but the fly is leaving instead.

12) **D** — The phrase means 'there will be no benefit in asking me'.

13) **sleeping** — 'awake' means 'conscious', whereas 'sleeping' means 'unconscious'.

14) **blunt** — 'spiky' means 'pointed', whereas 'blunt' means 'rounded'.

15) **cellar** — 'attic' means 'a room at the top of a house', whereas 'cellar' means 'a room at the bottom of a house'.

16) **enter** — 'exit' means 'to leave a place', whereas 'enter' means 'to come in to a place'.

17) **exterior** — 'inside' means 'inner part', whereas 'exterior' means 'outside'.

18) **lose** — 'find' means 'to recover', whereas 'lose' means 'to misplace'.

19) **saintly** — 'bad' means 'wicked', whereas 'saintly' means 'good'.

20) **satisfied** — 'hungry' means 'wanting food', whereas 'satisfied' means 'not wanting food'.

21) **failure** — a 'success' means 'a win', whereas a 'failure' means 'a loss'.

22) **endless** — 'limited' means 'restricted', whereas 'endless' means 'unrestricted'.

23) **morning** — 'evening' means 'the time at the end of the day', whereas 'morning' means 'the time at the start of the day'.

24) **even** — 'odd' means 'not divisible by 2', whereas 'even' means 'divisible by 2'.

25) **bless** — 'curse' means 'to wish someone ill', whereas 'bless' means 'to wish someone well'.

26) **sensible** — 'silly' means 'absurd', whereas 'sensible' means 'reasonable'.

27) **deny** — 'admit' means 'allow', whereas 'deny' means 'to refuse'.

28) **come** — 'go' means 'to move away from', whereas 'come' means 'to move towards'.

29) **walk** — 'Whenever we go for a **walk** in the woods'

30) **lecture** — 'Dad likes to **lecture** us on the surroundings.'

31) **brown** — 'Once it was on the way leaves turn **brown** in autumn'

32) **height** — 'we estimated the **height** and age of the biggest trees'

33) **going** — 'We're **going** to Brook Valley today'.

34) **groaned** — 'Mita and I **groaned**'

35) **where** — 'While Dad was trying to work out **where** we were'

36) **opposite** — 'Mita and I deliberately dashed off in the **opposite** direction'

37) **other** — 'racing each **other** to be first up the hill.'

38) **fainter** — 'We could hear Dad's shouts getting **fainter** in the distance'

39) **care** — 'but we didn't **care**'

40) **today** — 'we were determined that **today** was going to be fun!'

41) **change** — 'change' can mean 'to make different' or 'money in the form of coins'.

42) **rap** — 'rap' can mean 'a sharp knock' or 'a type of music'.

43) **fire** — 'fire' can mean 'to dismiss someone from a job' or 'the burning of fuel'.

44) **watch** — 'watch' can mean 'to look at something' or 'a device for telling the time'.

45) **vault** — 'vault' can mean 'to jump' or 'a safe'.

46) **down** — 'down' can mean 'the feathers of young birds' or 'in a lower place'.

47) **interested** — Both words mean 'eager to learn more'.

48) **drowsy** — Both words mean 'in need of sleep'.

49) **goblet** — Both are vessels that you drink from.

50) **tedious** — Both words mean 'uninteresting'.

51) **task** — Both words mean 'a duty'.

52) **concern** — Both words mean 'anxiety'.

53) **ailing** — Both words mean 'unwell'.

54) **towering** — Both words mean 'of great height'.

55) **possess** — Both words mean 'to be the owner of'.

56) **infant** — Both words mean 'a young child'.

Pages 48-53 — Assessment Test 4

1) **C** — In the passage it says "The afternoon sun was getting low", so it must be late afternoon.

2) **A** — Mole is "restless" — it is Rat who is "in a dreamy mood".

3) **C** — In the passage Rat says "Not yet, my young friend, wait till you've had a few lessons."

4) **B** — Mole was jealous because Rat was "sculling so strongly and so easily along".

5) **A** — Rat "fell backwards off his seat with his legs in the air", but he remains in the boat.

6) **D** — Mole doesn't hit Rat with the sculls.

7) **A** — 'Reckless' means 'impulsive' or 'not thinking of the consequences'. This accurately describes Mole's behaviour in these lines.

8) **C** — To feel "at home" somewhere means 'to feel comfortable'.

9) **B** — 'victorious' is closest in meaning to "triumphant". Both words mean 'having won something'.

10) **D** — 'panicked' is closest in meaning to "alarmed". Both words mean 'feeling afraid'.

11) **A** — 'Lying down flat' is closest in meaning to "prostrate".

12) **B** — This phrase means that Mole wanted to prove that he could row just as well as Rat.

13) **garage** — The other three are all rooms in a house.

14) **plate** — The other three are containers for drinking from.

15) **sow** — The other three are the young of animals.

16) **cloud** — The other three are types of precipitation.

17) **lady** — The other three are names for children.

18) **peer** — The other three are facial expressions.

19) **begin** — Both words mean 'to commence'.

20) **absent** — Both words mean 'not present'.

21) **decline** — Both words mean 'to lessen'.

22) **stingy** — Both words mean 'unwilling to spend money'.

23) **just** — Both words mean 'unbiased'.

24) **neat** — Both words mean 'ordered'.

25) **minute** — Both words mean 'very small'.

26) **obvious** — Both words mean 'easy to see'.

27) **B** — 'Hester crept through the **dense** undergrowth'

28) **A** — 'signalling to Benito, her cameraman, to **remain** silent.'

29) **A** — 'the forest was a treasure chest of filming **opportunities**'

30) **C** — 'she just hoped that today **would** be a good day.'

31) **B** — 'thorny vines gleefully tangled themselves **in** her mop of curly blonde hair.'

32) **A** — '**Parting** the emerald green fronds of the fragrant ferns'

33) **C** — 'A few metres **away** from her was a whole family of chimps.'

34) **A** — 'She couldn't believe her **luck.**'

35) **B** — 'Making sure **that** Benito was recording'

36) **A** — 'she turned breathlessly to **face** the camera.'

37) **C** — 'she **said** quietly to the camera.'

38) **B** — 'the large male is cracking the **hard** outer shells'

39) **C** — '**Meanwhile**, the female is grooming her infant'

40) **A** — 'the young chimp **closed** its eyes'

41) **B** — 'Its **mouth** was curved into a contented smile'

42) **A** — 'the chimp reminded Hester of her own son when he **was** a baby.'

43) **triumph** — 'lose' means 'to be unsuccessful', whereas 'triumph' means 'to be successful'.

44) **beneath** — 'above' means 'at a higher level', whereas 'beneath' means 'at a lower level'.

45) **borrow** — 'lend' means 'to give something as a temporary loan', whereas 'borrow' means 'to receive something as a temporary loan'.

46) **generous** — 'selfish' means 'acting for one's own benefit', whereas 'generous' means 'giving more than is necessary for other people's benefit'.

47) **antique** — 'modern' means 'new', whereas 'antique' means 'old'.

48) **retrieve** — 'misplace' means 'to lose something', whereas 'retrieve' means 'to get something back'.

49) **chef** — Both words mean 'someone who prepares food'.

50) **relax** — Both words mean 'to unwind'.

51) **rubbish** — Both words mean 'garbage'.

52) **trunk** — Both words mean 'a case for storing items'.

53) **kin** — Both words mean 'a family member'.

54) **gown** — Both words mean 'a frock'.

55) **scrumptious** — Both words mean 'delicious'.

56) **detest** — Both words mean 'to loathe'.

Pages 54-59 — Assessment Test 5

1) **C** — In the passage it says that Michael "stood in the freezing downpour".

2) **D** — The elephant is running away from the hunters who are chasing it.

3) **D** — In the passage the hunter says "It doesn't have tusks. No tusks means no ivory to sell".

4) **C** — Michael was "horrified" because the hunters were going to shoot the adult elephant and take her tusks to sell for ivory.

5) **B** — Michael is described as being "disorientated" — this shows that he is confused.

6) **B** — Michael realises that he has been back in time and has changed what happened in the past.

7) **A** — We only know that the name of the taller hunter is "Kevin".

8) **A** — 'flailed' is closest in meaning to "thrashed". Both words mean 'moved around violently'.

9) **student** — 'teacher' means 'someone who teaches', whereas 'student' means 'someone who learns'.

10) **left** — 'right' means 'the opposite of left', whereas 'left' means 'the opposite of right'.

11) **lengthy** — 'short' means 'brief', whereas 'lengthy' means 'long'.

12) **ancient** — 'young' means 'not old', whereas 'ancient' means 'old'.

13) **sullen** — 'jolly' means 'cheerful', whereas 'sullen' means 'sulky'.

14) **overpriced** — 'cheap' means 'inexpensive', whereas 'overpriced' means 'expensive'.

15) **imprison** — 'release' means 'to free', whereas 'imprison' means 'to lock up'.

16) **opaque** — 'see-through' means 'transparent', whereas 'opaque' means 'not see-through'.

17) **pliable** — 'brittle' means 'inflexible', whereas 'pliable' means 'flexible'.

18) **doctor** — a 'patient' is 'someone being given medical treatment', whereas a 'doctor' is 'someone who gives medical treatment'.

19) **thick** — 'thin' means 'narrow', whereas 'thick' means 'wide'.

20) **tight** — 'loose' means 'slack', whereas 'tight' means 'taut'.

21) **peace** — 'war' means 'conflict', whereas 'peace' means 'the absence of conflict'.

22) **useless** — 'functional' means 'with a purpose' whereas 'useless' means 'without a purpose'.

23) **below** — 'over' means 'above', whereas 'below' means 'under'.

24) **civil** — 'rude' means 'impolite', whereas 'civil' means 'polite'.

25) **superior** — 'junior' means 'lower in rank', whereas 'superior' means 'higher in rank'.

26) **chuckle** — 'cry' means 'to weep', whereas 'chuckle' means 'to laugh'.

27) **shrink** — 'grow' means 'to increase in size', whereas 'shrink' means 'to decrease in size'.

28) **lofty** — 'low' means 'not far from the ground', whereas 'lofty' means 'far from the ground'.

29) **D** — The passage says that Gabby beat Paul, but that Will beat Gabby. Since Julia and Paul finished at the same time, Julia must have finished after Will.

30) **B** — In the passage it says that the yellow and blue teams were tied for first place before the egg-and-spoon race. Since Amita won the egg-and-spoon race and she was from the yellow team, the blue team cannot have been the overall winners.

31) **C** — In the passage it says that Amita "knew she could beat her arch-rival", which shows she is confident.

32) **B** — In the passage it says that the playing field was "newly mown", so Gabby cannot have slipped on some long grass.

33) **quiet** — 'The alarm pierced the **quiet** of the fire station.'

34) **tingled** — 'Amanda's body **tingled** with excitement'

35) **moment** — 'this was the **moment** she had been training for!'

36) **scarlet** — 'Racing to the **scarlet** fire engine'

37) **felt** — 'Amanda **felt** apprehensive, yet confident.'

38) **after** — '**after** a few minutes'

39) **into** — 'the engine swerved **into** a car park.'

40) **blazing** — 'Amanda dashed into the **blazing** building'

41) **corridor** — 'she inched along the smoke-filled **corridor**.'

42) **bedroom** — 'Entering a **bedroom**, she saw a terrified child'

43) **window** — 'she smashed the **window**'

44) **waiting** — 'carried him down the **waiting** ladder'

45) **motivate** — Both words mean 'to fill someone with the urge to do something'.

46) **debris** — Both words mean 'the remains of something that has been destroyed'.

47) **abundance** — Both words mean 'more than enough'.

48) **reply** — Both words mean 'to respond'.

49) **pursue** — Both words mean 'to follow something in order to catch it'.

50) **omen** — Both words mean 'a hint of what is about to happen'.

51) **veer** — Both words mean 'to turn quickly'.

52) **select** — Both words mean 'to pick something'.

53) **segment** — Both words mean 'a portion'.

54) **gloomy** — Both words mean 'with little light'.

55) **command** — Both words mean 'to tell someone to do something'.

56) **preserve** — 'Both words mean 'to maintain'.

Answers

Pages 60-65 — Assessment Test 6

1) **A** — In the text it says Narcissus rejected his admirers because "he thought that none of them were good enough."

2) **B** — In the passage it says that nymphs are "divine creatures who kept the plants, trees and animals alive."

3) **B** — In the passage it says that Narcissus rejected Echo, which means he did not love her.

4) **C** — Echo's heart was broken by Narcissus, so she wanted to go somewhere away from him.

5) **D** — It was a reflection, so it disappeared when the water moved.

6) **A** — In the passage it says "The sun rose and set many times", showing that many days had passed. It also says that Narcissus "rapidly weakened and died" at the spring, so he couldn't have been there longer than a few weeks.

7) **D** — This story is a warning against being obsessed with your looks, as Narcissus fell in love with his reflection and died.

8) **D** — 'famous' is closest in meaning to "renowned". Both words mean 'well known'.

9) **C** — 'conceited' is closest in meaning to "arrogant". Both words mean 'thinking highly of yourself'.

10) **C** — 'enticed' is closest in meaning to "lured". Both words mean 'tempted'.

11) **B** — The phrase "to no avail" means 'without success'.

12) **A** — The phrase "pining for his love" means that he became obsessed with his love and refused to eat or sleep, so he wasted away.

13) **snowflakes** — The words can be rearranged into the sentence 'I am going outside to play in the snow.'

14) **mittens** — The words can be rearranged into the sentence 'My favourite hat is fluffy and purple.'

15) **track** — The words can be rearranged into the sentence 'Harry lost his way and got home very late.'

16) **eggs** — The words can be rearranged into the sentence 'The birds built a nest out of moss and twigs.'

17) **brother** — The words can be rearranged into the sentence 'Alisha is going into town to buy a birthday present.'

18) **sit** — The words can be rearranged into the sentence 'You have done nothing but play computer games all day.'

19) **trip** — 'trip' can mean 'a journey' or 'to catch one's foot on something'.

20) **spell** — 'spell' can mean 'a short amount of time' or 'witchcraft'.

21) **minute** — 'minute' can mean 'very small' or 'a short unit of time'.

22) **fast** — 'fast' can mean 'at high speed' or 'to go without food or drink'.

23) **hollow** — 'hollow' can mean 'without content' or 'a depression in the ground'.

24) **mould** — 'mould' can mean 'to form into a desired shape' or 'a layer of fungi'.

25) **lead** — 'lead' can mean 'a type of metal' or 'to guide someone'.

26) **desert** — 'desert' can mean 'infertile' or 'to neglect someone'.

27) **sink** — 'sink' can mean 'a basin where you wash yourself' or 'to move in a downwards direction'.

28) **incense** — 'incense' can mean 'a fragrant smell' or 'to enrage someone'.

29) **thrilled** — 'Jack was **thrilled** to get a metal detector'

30) **whole** — 'He spent the **whole** day planning his first outing'

31) **would** — 'He **would** pack a picnic'

32) **buried** — 'find some **buried** treasure!'

33) **dawn** — 'The next day he got up at **dawn**'

34) **until** — 'Everything went smoothly **until** he opened his bag'

35) **awful** — 'realised something **awful**'

36) **battery** — 'he had forgotten to bring the **battery** pack!'

37) **eat** — 'All he could do was **eat** his picnic'

38) **home** — 'wait for the bus **home**.'

39) **back** — 'But he vowed to come **back** the following day'.

40) **needed** — 'with everything he **needed**.'

41) **malice** — Both words mean 'ill will towards someone'.

42) **wicked** — Both words mean 'bad'.

43) **close** — Both words mean 'nearby'.

44) **praise** — Both words mean 'to give positive feedback'.

45) **anxious** — Both words mean 'nervous'.

46) **consent** — Both words mean 'to allow something'.

47) **together** — 'alone' means 'by yourself', whereas 'together' means 'with other people'.

48) **overdue** — 'early' means 'before the expected time', whereas 'overdue' means 'later than expected'.

49) **frown** — A 'smile' is a facial expression showing pleasure, whereas a 'frown' is a facial expression showing displeasure.

50) **windy** — 'still' means 'no wind', whereas 'windy' means 'lots of wind'.

51) **descend** — 'rise' means 'to move upwards', whereas 'descend' means 'to move downwards'.

52) **microscopic** — 'immense' means 'large', whereas 'microscopic' means 'tiny'.

53) **famished** — 'full' means 'satisfied', whereas 'famished' means 'hungry'.

54) **despise** — 'admire' means 'to respect deeply', whereas 'despise' means 'to feel hate or contempt'.

55) **wrinkled** — 'smooth' means 'to have an even surface', whereas 'wrinkled' means 'to have an uneven surface'.

56) **approximate** — 'exact' means 'precise', whereas 'approximate' means 'imprecise'.

Pages 66-71 — Assessment Test 7

1) **B** — The wolves recognise that it is a human baby, and a baby wolf is a cub.

2) **A** — New-born babies cannot walk, and in the passage it says the baby "could just walk".

3) **B** — Father Wolf picks the baby up carefully, so that "not a tooth even scratched the skin".

4) **B** — He is explaining that the child is defenceless.

5) **B** — In the passage it says that the baby pushed his way in amongst the cubs "to get close to the warm hide" and to take "his meal with the others".

6) **D** — Father Wolf may have seen human children before, but Mother Wolf says, "I have never seen one."

7) **B** — Tabaqui calls Shere Khan "My Lord". This shows that he is a follower of Shere Khan.

8) **D** — 'used to' is closest in meaning to "accustomed to". Both mean 'familiar with'.

9) **A** — 'skin' is closest in meaning to "hide" here — "hide" is an animal's skin.

10) **C** — 'shoved' is closest in meaning to "thrust". Both words mean 'pushed'.

11) **A** — Mother Wolf says "was there ever a wolf that could boast of a man's cub among her children?" This shows that she is proud.

12) **D** — In the passage Father Wolf carries the child gently as if he were carrying an egg.

13) **A** — 'The day had started cold but **bright**'

14) **D** — 'sharpening the edges of the trees **against** the sky.'

15) **B** — 'leaden clouds gathered **suddenly**'

16) **A** — 'The wind sprang from **nowhere**'

17) **B** — 'within minutes the countryside **was** obscured'

18) **D** — 'High **above** the village'

19) **C** — 'they had searched frantically for **shelter**'

20) **A** — 'he **dragged** her deeper into the forest'

21) **B** — 'the trees would **provide** some kind of break'

22) **D** — 'the icy winds and drifting **snow**.'

23) **A** — 'he had **seen** it'

24) **B** — 'the two children had **crawled** into the temporary protection of the cave.'

25) **C** — 'Alawa's tiny body **shook** violently'

26) **C** — 'the combined **warmth** of their bodies'

27) **A** — 'still **clutching** the bag of herbs'

28) **B** — 'they had been collecting in the **forest**'

29) **absurd** — Both words mean 'foolish'.

30) **request** — Both words mean 'appeal to someone to do something'.

31) **taunt** — Both words mean 'to ridicule'.

32) **applaud** — Both words mean 'to congratulate'.

33) **aggravate** — Both words mean 'to irritate'.

34) **solace** — Both words mean 'consolation'.

35) **press** — Both words mean 'to apply pressure to something'.

36) **indulge** — Both words mean 'to spoil someone'

37) **stream** — The other three are all bodies of still water.

38) **stereo** — The other three are all used with a computer.

39) **parasol** — The other three are all items for keeping dry in the rain.

40) **hymn** — The other three are all types of poem.

41) **India** — The other three are all countries in Europe.

42) **heart** — The other three are all joints in the body.

43) **talkative** — Both words describe someone who talks a lot.

44) **overseas** — Both words mean 'in another country'.

45) **livid** — Both words mean 'cross'.

46) **victor** — Both words mean 'champion'.

47) **echo** — Both words mean 'to say something again'.

48) **circular** — Both words mean 'ring-shaped'.

49) **clarify** — Both words mean 'to make clearer'.

50) **primary** — Both words mean 'coming earliest in a sequence'.

51) **confinement** — 'freedom' means 'liberty', whereas 'confinement' means 'captivity'.

52) **retreat** — 'advance' means 'to move forwards', whereas 'retreat' means 'to move backwards'.

53) **grant** — 'refuse' means 'to deny someone something', whereas 'grant' means 'to give someone something'.

54) **deliberate** — 'accidental' means 'by accident', whereas 'deliberate' means 'on purpose'.

55) **stubborn** — 'willing' means 'eager to go along with something', whereas 'stubborn' means 'unyielding'.

56) **inferior** — 'better' means 'more good', whereas 'inferior' means 'less good'.

Pages 72-77 — Assessment Test 8

1) **B** — The poem begins "I should like to..." which shows that the poet wants to do the things he describes.

2) **C** — The poet is describing different countries in the poem — he describes a different country as being under a different sky.

3) **A** — Produce sold at the markets has come from "near and far".

4) **D** — The flamingo is flying "before his eyes" and the crocodile is watching it.

5) **B** — These lines show that the cities are 'bustling', which means very busy.

6) **D** — The tiger is "Lying close and giving ear / Lest the hunt be drawing near". This means 'lying and listening in case the hunt comes'.

7) **A** — The only cities that are mentioned in the poem are described as very busy.

8) **C** — 'eating' is closest in meaning to "devouring". Both words mean 'consuming'.

9) **B** — 'The World Conker Championships **began** in 1965'

10) **A** — 'unable to organise a fishing trip **because** the weather was so bad.'

11) **D** — 'At a loss for a fun way to **spend** their day'

12) **B** — 'Since then, the **event** has grown'

13) **C** — 'huge crowds of **spectators**.'

14) **C** — 'The proceeds raised are **donated** to charity.'

15) **A** — 'two players take it in turns to **swing** their conker'

16) **D** — 'The winner is the player **who** manages to smash their rival's conker.'

17) **B** — 'The contest **operates** as a knockout'

18) **D** — 'until only one player **remains**.'

19) **A** — 'the winners of the men's and women's events are **crowned** King and Queen Conker.'

20) **C** — 'have come from as far **afield** as Austria'

21) **C** — In the passage it says that Alex is two. Rosie is a year older than Alex, so Rosie must be three. Rosie is four years younger than Theo, so Theo must be 7, not 8.

22) **D** — In the passage it says that Jo "didn't want to stir from the cosy living room", so she agrees to Theo's game so that she can stay in the living room where it's warm.

23) **B** — In the passage it says that there was a "blazing log fire", so Theo doesn't put the pencil case up the chimney because he doesn't want to get burnt by the fire.

24) **C** — In the passage it says that Alex had his eyes open but that "since he was only two Theo wasn't too concerned".

25) **rift** — Both words mean 'a separation'.

26) **ruse** — Both words mean 'an act or device intended to deceive'.

27) **dire** — Both words mean 'very bad'.

28) **hazard** — Both words mean 'danger'.

29) **talon** — Both words mean 'the sharp nail of an animal or bird'.

30) **mature** — Both words mean 'fully grown'.

31) **bound** — Both words mean 'to jump'.

32) **teeter** — Both words mean 'to sway'.

33) **seize** — Both words mean 'to grasp'.

34) **refuge** — Both words mean 'a safe place'.

35) **feign** — Both words mean 'to act as something you're not'.

36) **mute** — Both words mean 'not speaking'.

37) **ally** — 'enemy' means 'foe', whereas 'ally' means 'friend'.

38) **cheap** — 'dear' means 'expensive', whereas 'cheap' means 'inexpensive'.

39) **reserved** — 'sociable' means 'fond of company', whereas 'reserved' means 'shy'.

40) **ignorant** — 'wise' means 'knowledgeable', whereas 'ignorant' means 'unknowledgeable'.

41) **industrious** — 'lazy' means 'idle', whereas 'industrious' means 'hard-working'.

42) **trivial** — 'serious' means 'important', whereas 'trivial' means 'unimportant'.

43) **briefly** — 'forever' means 'permanently', whereas 'briefly' means 'for a short time'.

44) **stunted** — 'tall' means 'above average height', whereas 'stunted' means 'below average height'.

45) **reap** — 'sow' means 'to plant', whereas 'reap' means 'to harvest'.

46) **criminal** — 'legal' means 'permitted by law', whereas 'criminal' means 'not permitted by law'.

47) **ocean** — 'land' means 'earth', whereas 'ocean' means 'sea'.

48) **elevated** — 'low' means 'close to the ground', whereas 'elevated' means 'above the ground'.

49) **servant** — 'master' means 'a person in charge', whereas 'servant' means 'a person who serves a master'.

50) **forthcoming** — 'past' means 'something that has happened', whereas 'forthcoming' means 'yet to happen'.

51) **imitation** — 'real' means 'genuine', whereas 'imitation' means 'fake'.

52) **vague** — 'clear' means 'obvious', whereas 'vague' means 'not obvious'.

53) **copious** — 'few' means 'not many', whereas 'copious' means 'many'.

54) **entice** — 'repel' means 'to drive away', whereas 'entice' means 'to lure'.

55) **expose** — 'hide' means 'to conceal', whereas 'expose' means 'to reveal'.

56) **pessimistic** — 'hopeful' means 'expecting a positive outcome', whereas 'pessimistic' means 'expecting a negative outcome'.